EXPERIENCING GOD'S FAITHFULNESS IN JUDGMENT AND HOPE

A Study of Jeremiah, Lamentations,
and Ezekiel

Jack W. Hayford
with
Jack Hayford III

THOMAS NELSON PUBLISHERS
Nashville

Experiencing God's Faithfulness in Judgment and Hope
A Study of Jeremiah, Lamentations, and Ezekiel
Copyright © 1998 by Jack W. Hayford

Published in Nashville, Tennessee, by Thomas Nelson, Inc.

Printed in the United States of America
1 2 3 4 5 6 7 8 — 03 02 01 00 99 98

CONTENTS

Experiencing God's Faithfulness in Judgment and Hope (A Study of Jeremiah, Lamentations, and Ezekiel) is one of a series of study guides that focus exciting, discovery-geared coverage of Bible book and power themes—all prompting toward dynamic, Holy Spirit-filled living.

About the Executive Editor

JACK W. HAYFORD, noted pastor, teacher, writer, and composer, is the Executive Editor of the complete series, working with the publisher in conceiving and developing each of the books.

Dr. Hayford is Senior Pastor of The Church On The Way, the First Foursquare Church of Van Nuys, California. He and his wife, Anna, have four married children, all of whom are active in either pastoral ministry or vital church life. As General Editor of the *Spirit-Filled Life® Bible*, Pastor Hayford led a four-year project which has resulted in the availability of one of today's most practical and popular study Bibles. He is author of more than twenty books, including *A Passion for Fullness, The Beauty of Spiritual Language, Rebuilding the Real You*, and *Prayer Is Invading the Impossible*. His musical compositions number over four hundred songs, including the widely sung "Majesty."

About the Writer

JACK HAYFORD III is a scientific technician who has worked as a paper chemist. He is a chemistry graduate (with honors) from Azusa Pacific University in California and did his graduate work at Lawrence University in Appleton, Wisconsin, at the Institute of Paper Science and Technology. He is a member and actively involved in teaching in his local congregation, where he and his wife, Joann, serve. They have two children: Dawn and Jack IV.

Jack's teacher/scientist bent early manifested itself when, as a pastor's son, he taught himself New Testament Greek as a side hobby, along with his interest in chess and wrestling as a member of the Los Angeles High School Championship Team.

His deep interest in the Bible and theology made him an able assistant to his father during the editorial preparation of the *Spirit-Filled Life® Bible*, released by Thomas Nelson Publishers in 1991.

Of this contributor, the Executive Editor has remarked: "It's a privilege to be involved with Jack in exacting areas of Christian life and thought. His thoroughness of thinking gives his work a quality that will profit every student."

THE GIFT
THAT KEEPS ON GIVING

Who doesn't like presents? Whether they come wrapped in colorful paper and beautiful bows, or brown paper bags closed and tied at the top with old shoestring. Kids and adults of all ages love getting and opening presents.

But even this moment of surprise and pleasure can be marked by dread and fear. All it takes is for these words to appear: "Assembly Required. Instructions Enclosed." How we hate these words! They taunt us, tease us, beckon us to try to challenge them, all the while knowing that they have the upper hand. If we don't understand the instructions, or if we ignore them and try to put the gift together ourselves, more than likely, we'll only assemble frustration and anger. What we felt about our great gift—all the joy, anticipation, and wonder—will vanish. And they will never return, at least not to that pristine state they had before we realized that *we* had to assemble our present with instructions *no consumer* will ever understand.

One of the most precious gifts God has given us is His Word, the Bible. Wrapped in the glory and sacrifice of His Son and delivered by the power and ministry of His Spirit, it is a treasured gift—one the family of God has preserved and protected for centuries as a family heirloom. It promises that it is the gift that keeps on giving, because the Giver it reveals is inexhaustible in His love and grace.

Tragically, though, fewer and fewer people, even those who number themselves among God's everlasting family, are opening this gift and seeking to understand what it's all about and how to use it. They often feel intimidated by it. It requires some assembly, and its instructions are hard to comprehend sometimes. How does the Bible fit together anyway? What does

Genesis have to do with Revelation? Who are Abraham and Moses, and what is their relationship to Jesus and Paul? And what about the works of the Law and the works of faith? What are they all about, and how do they fit together, if at all?

And what does this ancient Book have to say to us who are looking toward the twenty-first century? Will taking the time and energy to understand its instructions and to fit it all together really help you and me? Will it help us better understand who we are, what the future holds, how we can better live here and now? Will it really help us in our personal relationships, in our marriages and families, in our jobs? Can it give us more than just advice on how to handle crises? the death of a loved one? the financial fallout of losing a job? catastrophic illness? betrayal by a friend? the seduction of our values? the abuses of the heart and soul? Will it allay our fears and calm our restlessness and heal our wounds? Can it really get us in touch with the same power that gave birth to the universe? that parted the Red Sea? that raised Jesus from the stranglehold of the grave? Can we really find unconditional love, total forgiveness, and genuine healing in its pages?

Yes. Yes. Without a shred of doubt.

The *Spirit-Filled Life® Bible Discovery Guide* series is designed to help you unwrap, assemble, and enjoy all God has for you in the pages of Scripture. It will focus your time and energy on the books of the Bible, the people and places they describe, and the themes and life applications that flow thick from its pages like honey oozing from a beehive.

So you can get the most out of God's Word, this series has a number of helpful features. Each study guide has no more than fourteen lessons, each arranged so you can plumb the depths or skim the surface, depending on your needs and interests.

The study guides also contain six major sections, each marked by a symbol and heading for easy identification.

    WORD WEALTH

The WORD WEALTH feature provides important definitions of key terms.

BEHIND THE SCENES

BEHIND THE SCENES supplies information about cultural beliefs and practices, doctrinal disputes, business trades, and the like that illuminate Bible passages and teachings.

 AT A GLANCE

The AT A GLANCE feature uses maps and charts to identify places and simplify themes or positions.

 BIBLE EXTRA

Because this study guide focuses on a book of the Bible, you will find a BIBLE EXTRA feature that guides you into the Bible dictionaries, Bible encyclopedias, and other resources that will enable you to glean more from the Bible's wealth if you want something extra.

 PROBING THE DEPTHS

Another feature, PROBING THE DEPTHS, will explain controversial issues raised by particular lessons and cite Bible passages and other sources to which you can turn to help you come to your own conclusions.

 FAITH ALIVE

Finally, each lesson contains a FAITH ALIVE feature. Here the focus is, So what? Given what the Bible says, what does it mean for my life? How can it impact my day-to-day needs, hurts, relationships, concerns, and whatever else is important to me? FAITH ALIVE will help you see and apply the practical relevance of God's literary gift.

As you'll see, these guides supply space for you to answer the study and life-application questions and exercises. You may, however, want to record all your answers, or just the overflow from your study or application, in a separate notebook or journal. This would be especially helpful if you think you'll dig into the BIBLE EXTRA features. Because the exercises in this feature are optional and can be expanded as far as you want to take them, we have not allowed writing space for them in this study guide. So you may want to have a notebook or journal handy for recording your discoveries while working through this feature's riches.

The Bible study method used in this series revolves around four basic steps: observation, interpretation, correlation, and application. Observation answers the question, What does the text say? Interpretation deals with, What does the text mean?—not with what it means to you or me, but what it meant to its original readers. Correlation asks, What light do other Scripture passages shed on this text? And application, the goal of Bible study, poses the question, How should my life change in response to the Holy Spirit's teaching of this text?

If you have used a Bible much before, you know that it comes in a variety of translations and paraphrases. Although you can use any of them with profit as you work through the *Spirit-Filled Life® Bible Discovery Guide* series, when Bible passages or words are cited, you will find they are from the New King James Version of the Bible. Using this translation with this series will make your study easier, but it's certainly not necessary.

The only resources you need to complete and apply these study guides are a heart and mind open to the Holy Spirit, a prayerful attitude, and a pencil and a Bible. Of course, you may draw upon other sources, such as commentaries, dictionaries, encyclopedias, atlases, and concordances, and you'll even find some optional exercises that will guide you into these sources. But these are extras, not necessities. These study guides are comprehensive enough to give you all you need to gain a good, basic understanding of the Bible book being covered and how you can apply its themes and counsel to your life.

A word of warning, though. By itself, Bible study will not transform your life. It will not give you power, peace, joy, comfort, hope, and a number of other gifts God longs for you to unwrap and enjoy. Through Bible study, you will grow in your understanding of the Lord, His kingdom and your place in it, but you must be sure to rely on the Holy Spirit to guide your study and your application of the Bible's truths. He, Jesus promised, was sent to teach us "all things" (John 14:26; cf. 1 Cor. 2:13). So as you use this series to guide you through Scripture, bathe your study time in prayer, asking the Spirit of God to illuminate the text, enlighten your mind, humble your will, and comfort your heart. He will never let you down.

My prayer and goal for you is that as you unwrap and begin to explore God's Book for living His way, the Holy Spirit will fill every fiber of your being with the joy and power God longs to give all His children. So read on. Be diligent. Stay open and submissive to Him. You will not be disappointed. He promises you!

Tears of Sorrow, Tears of Joy
(Jeremiah)

Jeremiah has been called the weeping prophet—and not without reason. No other prophet in the Old Testament expresses as much feeling or provides such a window into his inner thoughts and the turmoil of his soul. Jeremiah's career, from his call as a young man until his death, was marked with tragedy: the tragedy of good King Josiah's death, the tragedy of the apostasy of Judah, and the culminating tragedy of the fall of Jerusalem. Jeremiah had many reasons for weeping.

Yet not all of Jeremiah's tears were sorrowful, for the Book of Jeremiah also contains some of the most hope-filled prophecies concerning the restoration of Israel. Jeremiah reveals that even in the most difficult of circumstances the Lord provides an anchor in which we can trust—and the promise of a new covenant. After all the tears of sorrow, God's message of hope can bring tears of joy.

Lesson 1 / Trusting in a Troubled World

On September 30, 610 B.C., there was a total eclipse of the sun. This would be no more than astronomical trivia but for the fact that on that very day Nabopolassar and an army of Babylonians were facing the Medes in battle. The eclipse ended the fighting as the two armies were thrown into a panic. Nabopolassar formed an alliance with the Medes and turned against his overlords, the Assyrians. So it came to pass that the motions of the heavenly bodies were providentially used by God to bring the downfall of Assyria.

Thus has God woven His glorious plan throughout the tapestry of history. And God's plan includes *you*! For the same God who coordinated the politics of the people of earth with the motions of the spheres of heaven has a place for you in His plan. In this first lesson we will discover how the natural occurrence of an eclipse was used by God.

THE BACKGROUND OF JEREMIAH

Jeremiah began to prophesy during the reign of Josiah. This was a period in which the kingdom of Judah was experiencing a measure of renewal: the weakening Assyrian Empire was not an imminent threat, and Egypt was not strong enough to attempt to expand its sphere of influence up the Mediterranean coast. As a result, Josiah had a time of peace wherein to pursue reforms and expand the territory of Judah north into the former territory of Israel.

Read 2 Chronicles 34:1–7. How old was Josiah when he began to reign? (v. 1)

When did Josiah begin his campaign of reform? (v. 3)

Can you think of an explanation for why Josiah did not begin to reform Judah earlier?

What are some of the reforms which were carried out by Josiah? (vv. 3–5)

We see that Josiah was a righteous king who strove to reform Judah and restore the pure worship of God. He personally sought the Lord, and he humbled himself when he heard the Law of the Lord and realized how far Judah had strayed from it. So he made a covenant with the Lord to follow the Law, and he initiated a vigorous program of suppression of idolatry.

It was into this setting that Jeremiah came prophesying. But Jeremiah's prophecy was not one of great encouragement for the reforms which had been started. Read Jeremiah 3:6–10.

Who are the two "sisters" in this passage? (vv. 6, 7)

How did God divorce backsliding Israel? (v. 8)

How did the example of Israel affect Judah? (v. 8)

Jeremiah told Judah that the judgment of God would be visited upon them. In spite of the reforms sincerely undertaken by Josiah, the society of Judah was too far gone into idolatry for the reforms to have a lasting effect. Although the land was cleansed by Josiah's work, the hearts of the people were not changed. The time of Judah's freedom from outside interference was also coming to a close, and a new power was rising in Mesopotamia.

THE RISE OF BABYLONIA

Assyria, which had been the dominant power in the world for more than 200 years, was in a state of decline when the king, Saracus, appointed Nabopolassar to be the governor of Babylonia. Nabopolassar was a Babylonian, and the Assyrian king hoped that he could keep Babylonia within the empire by appeasing them with a leader from their own ranks. However, this plan backfired by the design of Almighty God. The aforementioned eclipse provided Nabopolassar with the opportunity to ally himself with the Medes and turn against Assyria.

The war against Assyria commenced at once, and Nineveh, the Assyrian capital, was besieged. In the third year of the siege, a springtime flood of the Tigris River washed out part of the city walls and opened a breach for the besiegers.

After the fall of Nineveh, the Babylonians moved next against the Egyptians. In a decisive battle, fought at Carchemish, the Babylonians crushed the Egyptians and began moving west like the unstoppable tide. They retook Syria that same year and moved into Judah where Nebuchadnezzar made King Jehoiakim his vassal. At this time (605 B.C.) the first deportation of Jews to Babylon took place. It was in the first deportation that Daniel and his companions were taken to Babylon; it is also from this date that many scholars reckon Jeremiah's seventy years of captivity.

This period in Judah's history is described in 2 Kings 23:34—24:17. Use that text to answer the following questions.

Who made Jehoiakim king? (23:34)

How long did Jehoiakim serve Nebuchadnezzar? (24:1)

What occurred when Jehoiakim rebelled? (24:2)

Why did the Lord want to destroy Judah? (24:3, 4)

Who reigned after Jehoiakim? (24:6)

What did Nebuchadnezzar do to the new ruler? (24:12, 13)

Who did Nebuchadnezzar deport to Babylon? Who was left in Judah? (24:14)

Who became the new king of Judah? (24:17)

 FAITH ALIVE

This was a dark period in the history of Judah. In fact, Jeremiah was even commanded not to pray for the nation any longer.

Jehoiakim rebelled after serving Nebuchadnezzar for three years. He may have thought it was a good time to rebel, since the army of Babylon was engaged in central Asia. But Nebuchadnezzar sent such warriors as he could spare, and they began raiding the countryside (2 Kin. 24:2).

As soon as he could, Nebuchadnezzar himself came with his army and besieged Jerusalem. This apparently occurred right at the end of Jehoiakim's life, so his son, Jehoiachin, seeing that he could not hold out against the forces of Babylon, surrendered to Nebuchadnezzar. The Babylonian king stripped Judah of most of its remaining wealth, and he deported all the army commanders, craftsmen, and smiths. His goal was to break the effectiveness of the army by removing its leadership and the economic base needed to support the army. It was in this second deportation (597 B.C.) that Ezekiel was taken to Babylonia.

THE PERSPECTIVE OF THE EXILES

Ezekiel was a younger contemporary of Jeremiah. He was about twenty-five years old when he was deported to Babylonia, and he began his ministry about five years later (Ezek. 1:1–2). From his writings we gain a glimpse into the thinking of the people of Judah who had gone into exile. However, the picture we see is not encouraging. Instead of humble repentance, we see the same stiff-necked pride, unwillingness to admit one's sin, and willingness to listen to false prophets which was simultaneously leading the remnant in Judah to their ultimate destruction.

Read Ezekiel 3:4–11.

To whom is Ezekiel being sent? (v. 4)

Give three reasons that the people will not hear Ezekiel. (v. 7)

Ezekiel is commanded to speak to the captives in the name of the Lord "whether they _____, or whether they _____" (v. 11). What inference do you draw from this statement?

Read Ezekiel 13:1–9.

What is the source of the prophecies of the foolish prophets? (v. 2)

What are the foolish prophets accused of **not** doing? (v. 5)

What will the judgment be upon the foolish prophets? (v. 9)

Read Ezekiel 14:1–8.

Who came to inquire of Ezekiel? (v. 1)

What does the Lord accuse them of? (v. 3)

What does the Lord direct the house of Israel to do? (v. 6)

What will be the judgment upon those who do not repent? (v. 8)

From these passages we get a picture of the Israelites of the Exile which shows them to be unteachable, hard-hearted idolaters. They would not hear Ezekiel because they would not hear the Lord.

"What idols are set up in your hearts?" God asks the elders of Israel. The same question is echoed throughout the Bible and speaks to us today as clearly as it did in Ezekiel's day. Our response to the idols we find in our hearts also needs to be the same as what Ezekiel called for: repentance.

THE LAST DAYS OF JUDAH

As Jeremiah in Judah and Ezekiel in Babylonia both continued to call for genuine repentance and declare that judgment was about to fall upon Jerusalem, events were moving toward the end of Judah as a nation. In the second deportation Nebuchadnezzar took King Jehoiachin to Babylon and placed Mattaniah on the throne, changing his name to Zedekiah. In the fourth year of Zedekiah's reign, he joined in a conspiracy with neighboring states to rebel against Babylonian rule.

The rebellion had predictable consequences. Nebuchadnezzar came against Jerusalem with his army and besieged it. The people of Jerusalem held out to the bitter end, for they knew that, this time, Nebuchadnezzar would show no mercy. But after a year and a half, famine was severe in the city and the walls were breached. Zedekiah fled by night but was captured and brought to judgment before Nebuchadnezzar. Zedekiah was forced to watch as his sons were killed, and then his eyes were put out and he was led away in chains to Babylon.

The Babylonians then totally destroyed Jerusalem, and Judah ceased being a nation. The judgments foretold by Jeremiah and Ezekiel had come to pass, and the final result of Judah's continual idolatry was visited upon her.

FAITH ALIVE

This initial lesson has primarily set out the historical setting of Jeremiah and Ezekiel. However, There are two specific lessons we should see:

First, the Lord is the God of history. The judgment which came upon Judah came through the action of the political powers which were vying for control at that time. But God's providential control of everything from the raising up of kings to the flooding of rivers caused the confluence of events which resulted in the downfall of Judah.

Second, the Lord requires personal accountability. One of the common themes of both Jeremiah and Ezekiel is that the Lord will judge each one for his sin. Although the nation of Judah, the last representative of God's working with the sons of Jacob as a nation, was in decline and finally succumbed to Babylon, God was still working with mankind. But now He was directing a greater focus upon the heart of the individual rather than the life of the nation.

In this initial lesson, how have you seen evidence of God's working with individuals and His requiring of individual responsibility?   •

Consider one of the examples you have seen and determine how that example can be applied to your own life.

As we study these books in greater detail, we will see that these lessons are echoed throughout these books. God is in control and He will judge the nations. Yet He also requires obedience and humility of the individual, and each person will also be judged.

Lesson 2/God's Faithfulness in Trials *(Jeremiah 1; 26—28; 36—38; 40—44)*

Discerning God's voice and relating His message to the people was the challenge faced by all true prophets. Like most of the prophets, Jeremiah was often controversial. But unlike other prophets, Jeremiah was accused of being a traitor. To be sure, other prophets frequently had kings who didn't like them or their message. But Jeremiah was accused of betraying the country and the people that he loved deeply.

We know more about Jeremiah than we do about any other prophet. In his writings Jeremiah tells us a great deal, not only about what was happening, but also about his own thoughts, feelings, and reactions to events. Thus we can identify with Jeremiah, and we can learn how to face hard times and trying events and trust God—even when things don't get better.

JEREMIAH'S CALL

Jeremiah was a young man when the Lord called him to be a prophet. And like many of us, he did not feel that he was qualified to do the work to which the Lord was calling him. But God assured him that He would be with him, and He told Jeremiah two things which he could hold on to through the many rough times which lay ahead.

Read Jeremiah 1 and answer the following questions.

When did Jeremiah begin prophesying? (vv. 2, 3)

When did God ordain Jeremiah to be a prophet? (v. 5)

What three things does God say regarding His relationship to Jeremiah before his birth? (v. 5)

What objection did Jeremiah give God? (v. 6)

List at least three ways in which God answered Jeremiah's objection (vv. 7–10).

What was the first vision that God gave to Jeremiah and what did it signify? (vv. 11, 12)

What was the second vision the Lord gave to Jeremiah and what did it signify? (vv. 13–16)

Why was Jeremiah not to be dismayed before the people of Judah? (vv. 17–19)

In this passage we see how God assured Jeremiah that he would be able to do what the Lord required of him. It is interesting to note that God's criteria of success are not the same as ours. God wanted obedience. He said to Jeremiah, "Just give the message that I give you. They won't like it, but I will be with you and deliver you." God's criterion of success for His people is simply obedience.

Jeremiah also was told that God had set him apart for his task even before he was born. This ought to give us great assurance, for the same God who called and ordained Jeremiah has called each one of us.

Like Jeremiah, we have each been called and prepared for a work. God's knowledge of us existed before the worlds, and His plan includes your work for the kingdom of God.

Although it may seem insignificant in the world's eyes, only God can measure what your obedience means to His goals.

Jeremiah was given two visions as a means of confirming the call of God. The first was a vision of a rod of almond.

WORD WEALTH

ready, *shaqad* (shah-*kahd*); Watching, waking, hastening, anticipating; to be sleepless, alert, vigilant; on the lookout; to care for watchfully. The verb occurs twelve times, including Psalm 127:1: "Unless the LORD guards the city, the watchman stays awake in vain." In Jeremiah 31:28, God promises to watch over His people with an intent to build and to plant. The present reference may best be understood by noting the linguistic connection between "waking" *(shaqad)* and "almond" *(shaqed)* in Hebrew. The almond is considered the "waker" in Hebrew thought, because it, of all trees, blossoms early, watching diligently for the opportunity to bloom. Thus in verses 11, 12, the linking of the vision of an almond branch and its interpretation is clear.[1]

God was saying to Jeremiah that the time was at hand. Jeremiah was not just going to be preaching about a distant threat of judgment; the time was coming fast. The people would see the fulfillment of Jeremiah's words.

The second vision spelled out the main thrust of the message which the Lord was giving to Jeremiah. Jerusalem, and all of Judah, would be overthrown by the enemies from the north because of their wickedness and idolatry. At the end of this second message God reiterates His call, "Go and speak! I will strengthen you for what you will face, and I will deliver you." Jeremiah would need great strength as he lived through the death throes of the kingdom of Judah.

THE OPPOSITION OF JEHOIAKIM

Jeremiah lived through the reigns of five kings, but two of the kings reigned briefly. So Jeremiah's ministry before the fall of Jerusalem can be separated into three periods based upon who was king. The early period of Jeremiah's ministry occurred during the reign of Josiah. Josiah was a good king who tried to reform Judah. During this period Jeremiah probably experienced little or no official opposition.

But after Jehoiakim became king, things changed.

Read Jeremiah 26.

From the information in Jeremiah 26 and lesson 1 in this book, in what year did this event probably take place? (v. 1)

What foreign power was in control of Judah at this time?

Why did the Lord send Jeremiah to the temple to prophesy? (v. 3)

Paraphrase the essence of Jeremiah's message in your own words (vv. 4–6).

Why does the Lord refer to Shiloh? What is the significance of Shiloh?

How did the people respond to Jeremiah's message? (vv. 8, 9)

What four groups of people are mentioned? Which groups took Jeremiah's side and which groups stood against Jeremiah? (vv. 8, 10)

Why did the priests and prophets say that Jeremiah deserved to die? (v. 11)

Why did the princes say that Jeremiah did not deserve to die? (v. 16)

What king and prophet do the elders use as an example of how they should act? (v. 18)

Why is the story about Urijah of Kirjath Jearim included here? (vv. 20–23)

What does the story of Urijah tell you about Jehoiakim's attitude toward the prophets as opposed to the princes' and elders' attitudes?

This chapter records the response to Jeremiah's prophecy which is called the Temple Address. Jehoiakim had just become king, but he was subject to a foreign power. The freedom and prosperity which Judah had enjoyed was now over.

At this time one would think that the people of Judah would be chastened, and they would be in the proper frame of mind to receive correction from the Lord. So the Lord sent Jeremiah to bring His word to the people. The Lord says that the temple and Jerusalem will be like Shiloh. Shiloh was the city where the ark of the covenant was originally kept when the children of Israel first settled in Canaan (see 1 Sam. 4:3). However, in the time of Jeremiah, Shiloh was in ruins.

The response of the people is interesting even though predictable. The priests and prophets (false prophets, obviously) stood against Jeremiah, but the princes ruled in Jeremiah's favor. The people apparently sided first with the priests and prophets, but switched over to the princes' view.

Their response shows how shallow the repentance of the people was during Josiah's reforms. Josiah had worked for years to turn Judah back to following Yahweh, but less than a year after Josiah's death the people are calling for Jeremiah's head because he dared to speak against the temple and the city.

Read Jeremiah 36 and 2 Chronicles 34:14–33.

When did Baruch read the scroll in the temple? (36:9)

What foreign power controlled Judah at this time?

Why did Baruch read the prophecy rather than Jeremiah?
(36:5)

How did Baruch end up getting an audience with the
princes? (36:11–14)

What was the response of the princes to the prophecy?
(36:16)

What were the instructions of the princes to Baruch?
(36:19)

How did King Jehoiakim receive the prophecy?
(36:22–24)

What was the Lord's response to Jehoiakim's action?
(36:28–31)

In the Chronicles passage, who read the scroll of the Law
to King Josiah? (34:18)

What was the response of Josiah to the reading of the
Law? (34:19–21)

With whom did the emissaries of the king inquire? (34:22)

What was the response of the Lord to Josiah's action? (34:26–28)?

How did Josiah respond to the message from the Lord? (34:29–33)

On the surface we have the obvious contrast of one king who heard the word of the Lord and repented and another king who did not. But the drama of this contrast goes deeper. These two incidents were only about eighteen years apart. Michaiah, who first reported to the princes, was the son of Gemariah, who was one of the three princes who implored the king not to burn the scroll. Furthermore, Gemariah was the son of Shaphan who had read the Book of the Law to Josiah when he repented. All of these men would have remembered the times of Josiah and his reforms; most of them would probably have remembered the day when the king renewed the covenant (2 Chr. 34:31). Some of the men may even have been present when the Book of the Law was read to Josiah. We can read about this turnabout in attitude from father to son, but these men saw it first-hand. They were watching a nation fall away from God, and they could not stop it.

This incident also took place at a critical time: at this time the Babylonians had just taken control of Judah. Once again the Lord was speaking at a time when uncertainty and flux in the political arena should have made the rulers more apt to hear. But Jehoiakim was particularly hard-hearted and stubborn. His actions show that, in spite of all the surrounding evidence to the contrary, he felt that **he** was in control. In his arrogance he ended up rebelling against Babylon and bringing about his own downfall and the second subjugation of the city.

JEREMIAH'S MINISTRY IN ZEDEKIAH'S REIGN

Jehoiakim's rebellion brought about another siege of Jerusalem, but he died before the city was taken. His son became king and was taken captive by Nebuchadnezzar (2 Kin. 24:12). The new king, who was set on the throne by Nebuchadnezzar, was Jehoiakim's brother, Mattaniah. Nebuchadnezzar changed his name to Zedekiah and left him to rule the poorest people of the land.

From the beginning of his reign, Zedekiah was instructed by the Lord through Jeremiah to submit to the rule of Nebuchadnezzar. But there were also false prophets who spoke of the downfall of Babylon and the return of the captives. Given the conflicting messages, Zedekiah listened to the one he liked.

Read Jeremiah 27 and 28.

Look at 27:1, 3, and 28:1. From these references when do you think these events happened? How do you explain the reference to Jehoiakim in 27:1?

What did the Lord command Jeremiah to do, and what message went with the action? (27:1, 2)

What is the basis upon which God says He may give the lands to whomever He wishes? 27:5)

What did Hananiah prophesy? (28:2–4)

What was Jeremiah's initial response to Hananiah? (28:6)

What did Jeremiah say was the evidence of a true prophet? (28:9)

What was the word of the Lord to Hananiah, and what happened to him? (28:13–17)

These events took place at the beginning of Zedekiah's reign, and the word of the Lord was not just for Judah, but also for the surrounding nations. Jeremiah pleaded for the people to submit and live peaceably under the rule of Babylon, but the false prophets contradicted him.

Hananiah the son of Azur prophesied of freedom for Judah. Jeremiah's response is instructive. He agreed with Hananiah. Jeremiah believed that the Lord had told him to make the yokes which he bore, but he also wished for peace and freedom for his people. Thus, when Hananiah spoke and broke the yoke off his shoulder, Jeremiah's response was, "Amen, I hope it's true, but we'll see."

Many times we are in a hurry to see the fulfillment of a promise we think the Lord has given us. And many times we become very defensive if anyone says anything which seems to contradict our expectations. We would be wise to learn from Jeremiah: the Lord will confirm His Word. We don't need to try and enforce it, and we don't need to defend God.

Zedekiah reigned for eleven years in Jerusalem. Toward the end of that period, after Judah had rebelled again against Nebuchadnezzar, the opposition to Jeremiah became the most intense. Yet through the hardships Jeremiah remained obedient to proclaim the Word of the Lord, and the Lord remained faithful to protect Jeremiah.

Read Jeremiah 37 and 38.

Why did the Babylonians break off their siege of Jerusalem? (37:5)

What was the word which Jeremiah spoke to the king? (37:7–10)

What happened to Jeremiah during the time the siege was lifted? (37:12–15)

How did the Lord protect Jeremiah when he was imprisoned? (37:21)

How do these chapters give evidence of the weakness of King Zedekiah?

Why did the princes want Jeremiah placed in the dungeon? (38:4)

How did the Lord protect Jeremiah? (38:8–13)

While Jerusalem was under siege by the Babylonians, Jeremiah attempted to leave Jerusalem to go back to his town. His preaching was well known, of course, and a captain watching the city gate arrested Jeremiah, accusing him of deserting to the Babylonians. This began one of the hardest times in

Jeremiah's life. He was imprisoned and accused of being a traitor, and, as the siege dragged on, the famine in the city became severe. Jeremiah continued to proclaim the message that the Lord had given him, and several times Zedekiah consulted with him. But Zedekiah was somewhat wishy-washy: he would consult with Jeremiah and help him, then he would let Jeremiah's enemies do whatever they wanted.

And Jeremiah had plenty of enemies among the rulers. The princes said that Jeremiah's message that the king of Babylon would take the city was disheartening the people. They wanted Jeremiah silenced, so they threw him into a deep pit, probable a well or cistern. But the Lord had a person there to watch out for Jeremiah. Ebed-Melech petitioned the king to allow him to take Jeremiah out of the pit, and the king consented. So Jeremiah remained confined in the court of the prison until the city fell.

AFTER THE FALL OF JERUSALEM

After the fall of Jerusalem, Jeremiah was released and allowed to go to Babylon or stay in Judah. He chose to stay, for he still loved his country and his people. So in this last period of Jeremiah's life he continued to minister to the remnant which was left after Nebuchadnezzar took most of the people into exile.

Read Jeremiah 40 and 41, and answer these questions.

To whom did Nebuzaradan attribute the fall of Jerusalem? (40:2) Why did he say Jerusalem had fallen? (40:3)

Who did the Babylonians set up as governor? (40:5)

What two groups are mentioned who returned to Gedaliah after he had become governor? (40:6, 7, 11)

Why did Gedaliah tell them to gather summer fruit? (40:10)

How does this passage show the care of the Lord for the remnant?

Who was involved in a plot against Gedaliah? (40:14)

Describe briefly how Ishmael carried out his attack (41:1–10).

What was the response of the other captains to Ishmael's act? (41:11, 12)

Why did the people want to flee to Egypt? (41:17, 18)

The Babylonians placed Gedaliah son of Ahikam in the position of governor over Jerusalem. Gedaliah told the people to submit to Babylonian rule and to gather fruit for food to last through the coming months, for grain had not been planted because of the war. But the Lord provided for the people, and favorable weather conditions had resulted in an abundance of fruit, wine, and oil.

However, not all the people were satisfied with the turn of affairs. Baalis, the king of Ammon, conspired to have Gedaliah and several of his officials assassinated. Now everyone in Jerusalem faced a dilemma: Would the king of Babylon take vengeance on them for the death of the governor? They asked Jeremiah what they should do.

Read Jeremiah 42:1 through 43:7.

What did the people promise to do in response to the word of the Lord? (42:5, 6)

Was the word of the Lord which Jeremiah gave a positive word or a negative word? (42:9–12)

Summarize the word which Jeremiah gave to the people (42:9–22).

Why did the word emphasize so heavily what would happen if they disobeyed?

How did the people respond to the word? (43:1–7)

This incident is tragically predictable. After all that the people had been through, after repeatedly seeing the results of disobedience, and after having dramatic confirmation of Jeremiah's words, the people still refused to hear the voice of the Lord. Furthermore, they now did not even have the bad excuse of being deceived by the false prophets. So they made up their own excuses: "Baruch has set you against us!"

The incident is made even more ironic by the fact that Jeremiah gave them a positive word. After years of telling the people that judgment and destruction were coming to Jerusalem, Jeremiah could finally say, "The Lord says you can stay in the land, and He will deliver you." But once again we see the stubbornness of sinful humans who are bent on having their own way.

Jeremiah went down to Egypt with a remnant of survivors from Jerusalem, probably not of his own volition. And he continued to proclaim the word of the Lord to the end of his life. Let's look at the last prophecies which Jeremiah recorded.

Read Jeremiah 43:8 to 44:30.

What action did the Lord have Jeremiah carry out to show the people that their attempt to run from Nebuchadnezzar had been in vain? (43:9)

This passage contains two distinct prophecies: one concerning Egypt and one concerning the Jews who had fled to Egypt. What did the Lord say to the Jews in Egypt? (44:2–14)

How did the people respond to this prophecy? (44:15–19)

With what god were the Jews involved in idolatry? (44:17) What worship practices are mentioned? (44:17–19)

BEHIND THE SCENES

Queen of Heaven—a fertility goddess to whom the Israelites, especially the women, offered sacrifice and worship in the days before the fall of the southern kingdom of Judah (Jer. 7:18; 44:17–19, 25). In the time of Jeremiah, many people in Jerusalem and other cities of Judah worshiped the queen of heaven. Their worship included burning incense and pouring out drink offerings to her (Jer. 44:17). This was obviously a form of idolatry, but it is not clear exactly which pagan god was worshiped.

All the running of the people had been in vain. Nebuchadnezzar would conquer Egypt, but worse was the fact that God would set Himself against them because of their continual rebellions. And, true to form, the people rejected the Word that the Lord gave through Jeremiah.

 FAITH ALIVE

We are not told in Scripture how or when Jeremiah died, but there are two ancient traditions which provide different accounts. According to an old Jewish tradition, Jeremiah and Baruch were taken to Babylon after Nebuchadnezzar conquered Egypt, but some of the early church fathers say that he was stoned by the people in Egypt. Whichever is true, we see in Jeremiah a man who was obedient and steadfast. Throughout his life he was faithful to the Lord, and he saw the faithfulness of the Lord to him in many deliverances. God's deliverance does not necessarily make things easy for us, but He brings us deliverance so that we can continue to obey Him.

How have you seen God's deliverance in your own life? Can you think of a time when God's deliverance allowed you to be obedient to God but did not make your outward situation easier?

Obedience is one of the key lessons we can learn from Jeremiah, but what other lessons have you learned from examining his life?

---

1. *Spirit-Filled Life® Bible* (Nashville: Thomas Nelson Publishers, 1991), 1056, "Word Wealth: Jer. 1:12, ready."

Lesson 3/Faithfulness Expressed in Judgment

(Jeremiah 2:1—3:5; 5; 7:1—8:3; 25:1–14; 29)

"Order in the court!"

Going to court is not something we look forward to, whether it's a traffic court, divorce court, or some criminal proceeding. Whether we are guilty of anything or not, we wince a little when they say, "Here comes the judge!"

Most of us have a negative view of judgment. We think of it as a harsh judge sitting behind the bench just waiting to throw the book at us. We need to get a clearer picture of how the ancient Hebrews looked at judgment. One way to do this is by examining the word "judge."

WORD WEALTH

judge, *shaphat* (shah-*faht*); One who judges, governs, passes down judgment, pronounces sentence, and decides matters. The root is *shaphat,* to "judge," "decide," and "pronounce sentence." Judgment is the balance, ethics, and wisdom, which, if present in a ruler's mind, enables him to govern equitably and to keep the land free from injustice. Judgment, when used of God, is that divine faculty whereby He runs the universe righteously, handing down decisions that will maintain or bring about a right state of affairs.[1]

So we see that judgment, being closely connected to God's righteousness, is also an aspect of God's faithfulness. God could not "keep faith" with His people if He could not enforce righteousness and make decisions in their favor. For the unrighteous, judgment means condemnation, but for those who seek righteousness, the judgment of God is their vindication. In Jeremiah the prophecies of judgment against the nation were the result of the unrighteousness of the nation. Jeremiah repeatedly said that the judgment would be withheld if the nation would listen and turn to the Lord.

EARLY PROPHECIES

The first part of the Book of Jeremiah contains prophecies which were given early in his ministry. Many of his first oracles were probably given while Josiah was king. This was a time of spiritual renewal, yet for most of the people the renewal was just the latest fashion in religion. It did not reach into their hearts.

Therefore, Jeremiah was already speaking of the coming captivity and desolation of the country. The Lord wanted the people to wake up and truly seek Him, and He was warning them about what the consequences of the status quo would be. But the people's hearts were hard and their ears were dull. Even the subjugation of the nation, first to Egypt and then to Babylonia, and the successive deportations of their countrymen were not enough to rouse them to repentance.

Read Jeremiah 2:1—3:5.

What opening question does the Lord ask of His people? (2:5)

What charge does the Lord bring against His people? (2:9–13)

What two evils were committed by the people? (2:13)

What foreign countries are alluded to in 2:14–16? (Clue: check v. 18)

In 2:14–19 what reason is given for the judgment which has come upon Israel? Who is responsible for bringing it upon Israel?

What three illustrations are used in 2:20–25? What is the main point of each of the illustrations?

Paraphrase verses 26 to 28.

In verses 29 to 32, what three things does the Lord say He has done or has been to Israel?

Because Israel says, "I have not sinned," the Lord will present His case against them (v. 35). In verses 2:33 through 3:5 what charges does the Lord lay against Israel?

In this passage we see the faithfulness of God in His love for His people *and* His faithfulness to His law. The passage begins with the Lord tenderly remembering His deliverance of Israel and the early days of Israel's walking with the Lord. And then He asks, "What injustice have I done? Why have you strayed from Me?" God shows His faithfulness by not casting off Israel when He had every right to.

The Lord continues by showing them what the fruit of their sin has been thus far. They have come under servitude to foreign powers. There is an important lesson to see in this statement: Our actions judge themselves. God has designed both the universe and our nature in such a way that certain actions will bring about their own penalties. That is what God is talking about when He says, "Your own wickedness will correct you, and your backslidings will rebuke you" (v. 19).

Israel had fallen far from the Lord and their shame was coming upon them. They would be ashamed of the gods they had turned to, and they would cry again to the Lord God for salvation. But God would reply, "Where are your new gods? Cry out to them, and see if they can save you."

Jeremiah continues with a scathing rebuke: Israel had become so wicked that the harlots could learn from her, and the evidence of her sins was openly displayed. They had turned time and time again to other gods, yet they expected the Lord to receive them back.

Thus we see that even with a righteous king pursuing reform, the hearts of the people remained far from the Lord. With warnings of judgment and anguish of soul, Jeremiah continued to call to the people (see 4:19–21), but the people had become hard as rocks.

Read Jeremiah 5 and answer the following questions.

In 5:1 God asks Jeremiah to seek for a righteous man in Jerusalem. God says that if anyone righteous is found, He will spare the city. What story in the life of Abraham is this reminiscent of?

Describe the condition of the people of Judah as shown in verses 2–5.

What aspect of the faithfulness of God is shown in verses 7–9?

Compare verses 10 and 11 with Jeremiah 11:16 and Romans 11:16–21. What ought we to learn from these verses?

The people say that Jeremiah's words are not from God (v. 12), but what judgment does the Lord pronounce upon them? (vv. 14–17)

What aspect of God's faithfulness is shown in verses 10 and 18?

How are the people of Judah contrasted with the sea in verses 22 and 23?

What lesson from chapter 2 is restated in verses 24 to 25?

In verse 28, what two things does God rebuke the people for not doing?

The people of Judah had certainly strayed from God—to the point that they denied that He was speaking through Jeremiah. "All this bad news couldn't be from God!" they exclaimed. But God answers by again affirming the message of judgment: The people of Judah will be devoured by a foreign nation. The people of Judah have departed from God—they are more defiant than the stormy sea! They do not honor the Lord who provides, and their sin brings its own judgment by withholding good. "They do not plead the cause of the fatherless," and "the right of the needy they do not defend" (v. 28). Throughout the Bible the righteous are enjoined to aid the poor, the widows, the fatherless. These were the people who had little or no protection in ancient society. God expects no less of us today. In our desire to care for the souls of the lost, we can never afford to overlook their physical needs as well (see James 2:15, 16; 1:27).

THE TEMPLE ADDRESS

In the last lesson we examined some of the events in Jeremiah's life, and we looked at the occasion of his sermon in the temple. We saw that that message came at a time when the people ought to have been penitent, but instead, the sermon almost cost Jeremiah his life. What was said which stirred up the people so much? Let's look at the Temple Address and see.

Read Jeremiah 7:1 to 8:3.

How does the message from God to the people begin? (7:3) Is this a positive or a negative beginning?

In what ways are the people told specifically to amend their ways? (7:5, 6)

What are the people doing which the Lord calls "trust[ing] in lying words"? (7:9, 10)

What place does God use as an illustration of His message? (7:12)

What will be the results of non-repentance? (7:14, 15)

To whom is verse 16 addressed? How does it fit in with the rest of the message?

What does verse 18 show?

Summarize the message of verses 21 to 27.

According to verses 28 to 31, what sins have the people of Judah committed which are leading to destruction?

In your own words, describe the judgment which is coming upon Judah because of their unfaithfulness and sins.

God's patient mercy was evident in Jeremiah's time. At the beginning of the Temple Address, God is still saying, "I will let you remain in the land, if you repent." Thus, Jeremiah begins his address with hope. But that hope is tempered with the truth: You cannot continue to trust a lie. Just because the temple of the Lord is here does not mean that judgment will be withheld.

But the people are specifically told how to change and what evils need to be corrected. God has designed for us to live in community. We cannot be whole when our society is not whole. We must stand against injustice and oppression. Like Jeremiah, we are told to speak out for righteousness.

God's call for the correction of external evils also shows that we are whole persons. Our internal thoughts, feelings, and attitudes **will** be shown in our actions. One can only be a hypocrite with limited success because one's true feelings have a tendency to slip out. Jesus went right to the point when He said, "out of the abundance of the heart the mouth speaks" (Matt. 12:34). Thus, to truly effect a change in society, people need to change. This is why social activism, by itself, will never be enough.

The people of Jeremiah's day had come to believe that they were free to commit evil because the temple of the Lord guaranteed their safety. But God says, "Go to Shiloh and see what happens when wickedness is not turned away from." The judgment which was coming upon Judah would be the same as the judgment which came upon Israel.

Verses 21 to 27 show the people were still carrying out the sacrifices as the Law required. But God says, "You are missing the point! When I brought Israel out of Egypt, before I gave them the Law, I commanded obedience." The formal, ritualized practice of the temple worship was meaningless without the obedience which came from the heart. God had tried to tell the people this over and over through His prophets, but the people did not listen.

So the Lord again enumerates the sins of the nation: they have not obeyed (v. 28), they have not received correction (v. 28), there is no truth (v. 28), they have done evil (v. 30), they have polluted the temple (v. 30), they have built the high places (v. 31), they have sacrificed their children (v. 31). Because of all this sin, the Lord will destroy the people and cast them from the land. The people will be slaughtered and their bodies will be desecrated. The people had trusted in the temple instead of trusting in the Lord. Indeed, they had trusted in the temple while turning away from the Lord, so the Lord had to bring judgment in order to be faithful to His word.

THE BABYLONIAN EXILE

One of the best-known prophecies in Jeremiah is the prediction that Judah would go into captivity for seventy years. This prophecy was cited by Daniel as being the reason he set himself to pray for the restoration of the Jews to their land (Dan. 9:2), and it provides a significant example of fulfilled prophecy. Jeremiah himself told the people in Judah of this judgment, and, by means of letters, he also informed the Jews already in exile of the duration of the captivity.

Read Jeremiah 25:1–14.

When was this message given and how long had Jeremiah been prophesying? (v. 3)

Summarize the message which Jeremiah and all the prophets had been giving to the people (vv. 5–7).

What is to be the result of the failure of the people to listen to the word of the Lord? (vv. 8–11)

What will happen after the seventy years are complete? (v. 12, 13)

Look at the remainder of chapter 25. Who is prophesied against in the last part of the chapter?

The significance of the Babylonian captivity cannot be overstated, for it was that experience which finally taught God's people to stay away from idolatry. After the return from exile, the Jews never again went back to pagan worship, for they knew that it was their repeated turning to false gods which had led to the Exile.

Jeremiah and the other prophets had been giving essentially the same message: repent, and turn away from false gods. But from the times of the judges, more then five hundred years earlier, the people had not listened. Therefore, the Lord was going to bring about the destruction of the nation, and for seventy years the people would learn that God, who is faithful, expects us to be faithful.

After the seventy years are completed, God says He will judge Babylon. And in fact, the remainder of the chapter speaks of judgment upon the nations of the world. If God brings punishment upon His own, then the ungodly shall most certainly also be judged.

THE LETTER TO THE CAPTIVES

Read Jeremiah 29.

When was this letter sent? (vv. 2, 3)

In what verse does the letter end?

The Lord says that He caused the people to be carried into captivity (v. 4). Why does the Lord want to make that point, and what message ought the captives hear from that statement?

What does the Lord tell the people to do? (vv. 5–7)

What does the Lord tell the people **not** to do? (v. 8)

Verses 10 to 14 form a beautiful passage which is full of hope and blessing. List several things which are promised in this passage.

Why does the Lord preface the message about the impending judgment of Judah with a statement about prophets in Babylon? (v. 15)

Summarize the message concerning the judgment of the people remaining in Judah (vv. 16–20).

This letter names three false prophets (vv. 21, 24). Who are they?

What judgment will come upon the false prophets? (vv. 21, 22, 32)

What differences do you see between the first two false prophets and the last one? Why do you think these differences occur?

This letter was sent early in the reign of Zedekiah with messengers which Zedekiah had sent to Babylon. It was probably sometime in the first four years of Zedekiah's reign, for we know that Zedekiah himself went to Babylon in the fourth year (Jer. 51:59), and his messengers probably went to Babylon prior to his visit. Therefore, this letter was written between seven and eleven years after the prophecy in chapter 25.

In the beginning of the letter God says that He has caused the captivity to occur. This statement of God's control of events is both sobering and hopeful. First, it should have made the people realize that this captivity was truly God's punishment upon their sin. God had warned them repeatedly through the prophets; He had given them ample opportunity to turn from their sin. But they had continued in rebellion, and now the judgment had come.

Beyond that sobering reality, however, lay a message of hope. God was in control—not their captors. He was still with them and He desired to give them peace in the place where they were. Thus the Lord tells the people to settle down, build and plant, and seek the good of the city where they live, "for in its peace you will have peace" (v. 7).

Along with the command to settle in for an extended period is the warning against false prophets. If a prophet says that the captivity will be brief, then he is not prophesying truly.

Right on the heels of the prophecy that they will be in captivity for seventy years, however, comes the promise that the Lord will visit them and cause them to return to the land of their forefathers. And then the Lord makes one of the most hope-filled statements in this book, "I know the thoughts that

I think toward you, says the Lord, thoughts of peace and not of evil, to give you a future and a hope" (v. 11). How hopeful that statement must have been for those Jews who had just recently been deported to a strange land! And God continues with promises that He will hear their prayers and gather them back to their land.

But Jeremiah returns again to the warning against the false prophets, addressing two false prophets by name: Ahab and Zedekiah. Jeremiah predicts that they will be slain by Nebuchadnezzar because they have spoken a lie in the name of the Lord and committed adultery.

Jeremiah also speaks of Shemaiah at the end of this passage. Shemaiah had written to Zephaniah, the priest in Jerusalem, asking why Jeremiah was not being punished. Since he wrote to the priests, and gave advice to the high priest, he was probably a priest who had held a high position prior to the Captivity.

But God is not a respecter of persons. Regardless of the position which Shemaiah had held, he was now in rebellion against God, and God would judge him. Neither Shemaiah nor any of his family would see the deliverance which the Lord would accomplish at the appointed time.

    FAITH ALIVE

This lesson has God's faithfulness in judgment. God's holiness demands a response to sin which reveals both the true nature of sin and the true nature of God. God is perfectly holy and just. Furthermore, He is the Judge of the universe and He cannot compromise His law or the principles on which the universe was founded. Sin, on the other hand, is a total rejection of God and all that God is. Sin rejects holiness, justice, law, and life itself.

The other side of judgment, however, stresses that God is merciful and seeks the good of His people. Just as the people of Judah were promised that the judgment would be stayed if they repented, and just as the captives were promised that they had a future, we have been given "great and precious promises" (2 Pet. 1:4) for our future which include nothing less than partaking of God's nature.

In this lesson, which of Jeremiah's judgment prophecies spoke to you most personally? Why?

What have you learned about God and His judgment from this lesson?

How will this impact your everyday life and how you think about the world?

1. *Spirit-Filled Life® Bible* (Nashville: Thomas Nelson Publishers, 1991), 349, "Word Wealth: Judg. 2:18, judge."

Lesson 4/The Faithful Teaching of the Lord
(Jeremiah 13; 18—19; 35)

One of the teaching tools which has been used throughout time is the illustrated message. Through the prophets and teachers of Israel, God repeatedly used graphic illustrations or acted out lessons to make a point. So we find Jeremiah using illustrated messages under the guidance of the Lord. (Watch for them as you continue through this study.) The message which Jeremiah proclaimed was the same, but by illustrating the message in different ways the force of the message was fresh and the call for repentance came out clearly once again.

THE LINEN SASH

Read Jeremiah 13:1–11.

What is the significance of the fact that the sash is made of linen?

What was Jeremiah told *not* to do with the sash? (v. 1)

Where did God tell Jeremiah to take the sash? (v. 4)

What happened to the sash? (v. 7)

In this "acted prophecy" which Jeremiah performed before the people of Judah every part of the action had significance. What is the significance of the following:
The fact that Jeremiah was not to put the sash in water? (v. 1)

Hiding the sash by the Euphrates? (v. 4)

The fact that the sash was ruined? (v. 7)

 PROBING THE DEPTHS

Jeremiah was told to take the linen sash to the Euphrates River and hide it. Then after many days he was to return to the Euphrates and recover the sash. How did this action relate to God's message? The Lord says, "*In this manner* I will ruin the pride of Judah and the great pride of Jerusalem" (13:9, italics added). The manner in which the sash was ruined was by being removed from the land of Israel and taken to the Euphrates. This symbolism, referring to the Lord removing the people beyond the Euphrates, is both direct and powerful.

The sash clearly represents the people of Israel. God says that He wanted Israel to cling to Him so that they would be His people for praise and glory (13:11). The significance of the fact that it was a linen sash also relates to the people bringing praise and glory to God, for linen was the material from which the garments and sashes of the priests were made.

Jeremiah was commanded not to wash the sash, because the people, likewise, were not being washed. The people of Judah were living in their sins, and they were not repenting. Therefore, the Lord was going to remove Judah and Jerusalem in order to ruin their pride.

Read Jeremiah 13:12–27.

What was the meaning of the full wine bottles? (v. 13)

What will be the end result of the pride of Judah? (v. 17)

Why is the queen mother mentioned in verse 18 rather than the queen?

To whom does this prophecy refer as the ones who will take Judah captive? (v. 20)

What is the significance of the heels being made bare? (v. 22)

Comment on the reference to "lustful neighings" in verse 27. Compare Jeremiah 5:8.

Jeremiah's message again is that the nation will go into captivity if they do not turn from their pride. The reference to the queen mother indicates the influence that she carried. The king usually had several wives and concubines, but he only had one mother.

The remainder of the prophecy tells about how Judah will be scattered and shamed. The statement that the heels are made bare is unique to Jeremiah. It is probably referring to the fact that the captives would be led away barefooted, suffering exposure and abuse.

The Lord ends this word by saying that the sins and adulteries of Judah would end with their destruction. Yet with all the wickedness which Judah had committed, God was still pleading with her to come back and be made clean.

THE POTTER AND THE CLAY

Read Jeremiah 18, paying particular attention to the incongruity of the word of the Lord and the people's response.

What is the chief message that the Lord is trying to communicate through this prophecy?

How did the people respond to the lesson of the potter and the clay? (v. 12)

What question does the Lord ask "among the Gentiles"? (vv. 13, 14)

What is the essence of the second message which the Lord gives the people? (vv. 13–17)

How do the people respond to Jeremiah's second message? (v. 18)

The lesson of the potter and the clay is perhaps the most memorable in all of Jeremiah. The Lord says that a nation, or a person, that He has doomed for destruction because of their wickedness can repent and turn from their evil. If they do so, the Lord *will* relent and not bring judgment upon them.

This is the picture God wants us to see—not only that Judah had turned away from what was true and wholesome, but that we have a tendency to do the same. Whenever we turn away from our true life-source we are behaving just as the people of Judah did.

But we can take hope in the patience of God. He bore with Israel for years; He called them to repentance in spite of their refusals to hear Him. So in your struggles with your own sin, hope in the patience and goodness of God. If He bore so long with the outright rebel, He will have patience with a weak child.

THE POTTER'S FLASK

Read Jeremiah 19.

Where is this prophecy acted out? (v. 2)

To whom does Jeremiah give this message? (v. 1)

What reasons does the Lord give for bringing catastrophe on Jerusalem? (vv. 4, 5)

What action does Jeremiah perform, and what is the meaning of the action? (vv. 10, 11)

After giving this prophecy, where does Jeremiah go and what does he do? (vv. 14, 15)

A second time the Lord told Jeremiah to go to the potter, this time to get a vessel with which to show the people the word of the Lord. Jeremiah took some elders of the people and priests and went to the Potsherd Gate by the Valley of the Son of Hinnom.

WORD WEALTH

Elders, *zaqen* (zah-*kayn*); an elder, old man, aged person. The verb means "to become old." Older persons are respected in Scripture because their experience in life has brought them wisdom.[1] It is significant that the elders were men, like Jeremiah, who would have remembered the reign and reforms of Josiah, and who had seen firsthand the decline of the nation of Judah.

BEHIND THE SCENES

"The Valley of Hinnom—a deep, narrow ravine west and south of Jerusalem. At the high places of Baal in the Valley of Hinnom, parents sacrificed their children as a burnt offering to Molech (2 Kin. 23:10). Ahaz and Manasseh, kings of Judah, were both guilty of this awful wickedness (2 Chr. 28:3; 33:6). Apparently, the Valley of Hinnom was used as the garbage dump for the city of Jerusalem. Hinnom thus became a graphic symbol of woe and judgment and of the place of eternal punishment called hell."[2] This location was an appropriate backdrop for Jeremiah's message.

The Lord begins this word with three main charges: Judah has forsaken the Lord, they have turned to other gods, and they have built the high places where innocent blood is shed. During the reign of Josiah the high places of Baal had been destroyed. As soon as Josiah was gone, the high places were rebuilt.

Because of the wickedness into which the people had descended, the judgment is about to come upon them. The valley will be filled with the bodies of the guilty, and the city will be destroyed. As a sign of the finality of this judgment, Jeremiah broke the potter's vessel in the sight of the witnesses he had brought to the gate, and he said, "This is how the city will be broken—it will be shattered irreparably." Then he went back to the temple and gave the same message to the rest of the people.

This message came without mentioning the possibility of averting the judgment. Judah had fallen beyond hope, and the destruction of the nation was now certain.

THE SIGN OF THE RECHABITES

Read Jeremiah 35.

When did this incident occur? (v. 1)

Describe the lifestyle of the Rechabites (vv. 6–10). Were they Jewish? Why did they follow their particular lifestyle? How long had their family been living thus?

What did Jeremiah tell the Rechabites to do and what was their response? (vv. 5, 6)

How does the Lord use the example of the Rechabites to give a message to Judah?

What does the Lord promise to the Rechabites? (vv. 18, 19)

The Rechabites were nomadic Jews who came into Jerusalem during the siege by Nebuchadnezzar at the end of Jehoiakim's reign. They had been faithfully following the commands of their ancestor for 250 years (see 2 Kin. 10:15, 23). Thus, when Jeremiah offered them wine they refused, for they still held to the directives given by their forefather, Jonadab.

The example which the Lord gave Judah in the Rechabites was positive: They were a sterling example of faithful obedience. But the message the Lord gave was not so positive: "If the Rechabites can obey their forefather, why can't you obey God!" The Lord again condemns Judah for their disobedience and announces impending judgment on Jerusalem.

As for the Rechabites themselves, the Lord promises that their family will always have a man who stands before the Lord in service. This provides another example, from many in the Bible, which show that honoring one's parents provides blessing and carries its own rewards.

FAITH ALIVE

This lesson on "The Faithful Teaching of the Lord," has an important lesson on the nature of God. He is being faithful by His teaching of us, and He teaches us in a way that will communicate the message truly, memorably, and forcefully.

God's faithful teaching did not end with Jeremiah, nor with the New Testament. The Lord still teaches us today— both by illuminating His Word and teaching us from redemptive history, and by illuminating our hearts and minds by His Holy Spirit—using everyday events in our lives to teach us.

What has the Lord used in His Word which has been an especially memorable lesson to you?

What has the Lord used in your own life to give you an especially memorable lesson?

1. *Spirit-Filled Life® Bible* (Nashville: Thomas Nelson Publishers, 1991), 860, "Word Wealth: Ps. 119:100, ancients."

2. *Nelson's New Illustrated Bible Dictionary* (Nashville: Thomas Nelson Publishers, 1995), 568, "Hinnom, Valley of."

Lesson 5/Trusting the Lord of the Nations
(Jeremiah 46—51)

God's name never appears in the Book of Esther, but a careful reading of this story reveals His hand at work in the lives of Esther, Mordecai, and even the evil Haman. Through circumstances which God controlled, even in a country hundreds of miles from the Jewish homeland, a major holocaust was averted.

God is the Lord of the nations. And He proves it in His providential control of history and in His judgment of the nations as proclaimed by His prophets. In this lesson we will look at Jeremiah's prophecies against other nations around Judah, and we will see how God's faithfulness extends to His rulership of the whole world.

JUDGMENT ON EGYPT

Read Jeremiah 46:1–12.

When was this prophecy given and to what battle does it relate? (v. 2)

Was this message given by Jeremiah before or after the battle? Upon what evidence in the text do you base your decision?

Verse 5 asks, "Why have I seen them dismayed and turned back?" What answer is given?

To what is Egypt likened in this passage? (vv. 7, 8) How is that illustration particularly suited to Egypt?

Verses 6 and 12 both spell out the fate of Egypt. What do they say which is similar? What do they say differently?

This is the first of two prophecies against Egypt in chapter 46 of Jeremiah. The prophecy concerns the battle of Carchemish in 605 B.C. which is recognized as one of the most important battles of ancient times. Jeremiah probably gave this prophecy shortly before the battle itself.

The prophecy begins with a call to arm for battle. The weapons are brought forth and made ready, but in spite of the magnificence of the appearance of the army, their power is broken and they flee because fear strikes them (v. 5). Egypt came in like the rising tide of the Nile. But the Lord proclaims that it is He who is in control; He has called Egypt to His sacrifice (v. 10).

Verses 6 and 12 tell of Egypt's defeat. Both verses indicate that the mighty man will fall. The mighty men were the elite of the army. Their courage and strength formed the backbone of the army. Thus, saying that the mighty have stumbled and fallen is an indication that the heart of the force was overcome. Verse 6 tells us that the swift will not escape; this continues the thought of verse 5 which says that Egypt's army was turned back and fled. On the other hand, verse 12 says that the nations have heard of the defeat of Egypt. News of its defeat will be heard throughout the world.

This should have served as a warning to the rulers of Judah not to put their trust in Egypt. This prophecy also shows that the Lord is the God of the nations. Egypt had plans to "go up and cover the earth" (v. 8). But the Lord has an appointment for Egypt, and it is not the one that Egypt has planned.

Read Jeremiah 46:13–28.

In verses 14–17 what expressions are used which are similar to expressions in the previous prophecy? What indications are there that this prophecy relates to the land of Egypt itself and not just a defeat of the army as in the previous prophecy?

What statements does Jeremiah make in this prophecy which indicate God's control of events? (vv. 15, 16, 18, 23)

Verse 18 says, ". . . he shall come." Who is "he"?

Who is Amon of No? (v. 25)

Summarize verses 27 and 28.

This passage spells out the fate of Egypt. What was begun with the defeat of the Egyptian army at the Euphrates River would culminate with the conquest of Egypt itself. Jeremiah begins by declaring that this word is to be heard in Migdol, Noph, and Tahpanhes. These were all cities of the delta region in Egypt, indicating that the entire region would be overthrown by Babylon.

Jeremiah again uses strong picturesque expressions of the devouring sword and the Egyptian soldiers falling against one another as they are swept away in defeat. But notice that the prophet didn't mention Nebuchadnezzar or the Babylonians by name. His purpose in not naming the conquerors of Egypt is that he wants to emphasize that this is the Lord's doing. The Lord is God over all the nations of the earth—even the greatest. And the kings of the earth carry out the bidding of the Lord.

In verses 25 and 26 Jeremiah reinforces his poetic prophecy in prose. Amon was the sun god of the Egyptians, and No was the ancient capital city, also called Thebes. So Egypt will be overcome, and none of her gods will help her.

Jeremiah ends his prophecy against Egypt with a word of hope for Israel. The Lord tenderly says to His people, "Don't be afraid, for I will save you. You will not be in captivity forever, for I will bring your children back to your land. But, all the nations which have oppressed you will be destroyed." Note the very last words of the prophecy, "I will rightly correct you, for I will not leave you wholly unpunished" (v. 28). Christ has taken the ultimate penalty for our sins. By dying on the Cross, He saved us from an eternity apart from God. But God is also interested in developing us into His image, and that frequently requires correction. We need to recognize and accept the correction of the Lord and learn to be conformed to His image, for that is the goal toward which we press (Phil. 3:7–14).

THE FIRST PROPHECY AGAINST BABYLON

Read Jeremiah 50.

This prophecy is about the judgment of Babylon, but within it are several places where the prophet addresses the children of Israel. What sections in this prophecy are promises to Israel rather than words of judgment on Babylon?

Restate verse 7 in your own words. How do people today use similar excuses for their own actions?

In this chapter at least four specific reasons are given for the judgment of Babylon. List the reasons you find (vv. 11, 17, 18, 24, 29).

According to this prophecy, who will the Lord use to judge Babylon? (vv. 3, 9, 41)

In verse 12 and following, who is "your mother"?

Verses 11–13 and verses 39 and 40 are similar in content. Has this part of the prophecy been fulfilled? If so, when and how?

Verses 17 through 20 are one section which includes a promise to Israel. How is this word to Israel different from the first one? (vv. 4–5) How does this promise expand on what was said in the first word?

The third section which addresses Israel is in verses 33 and 34. How does this promise build on what was said before?

Notice Jeremiah's interesting insight into how people excuse their own sins. He says that the nations who oppressed

Israel said that they had done nothing wrong because Israel had sinned. This tendency to excuse our own behavior because of another's failure is deeply ingrained in our fallen human nature. But our neighbor's sin does not excuse our own. Ultimately we are all measured against the changeless standard of God's character and holiness.

Jeremiah declares that Babylon will be uninhabited and desolate because they rejoiced in the destruction of Israel (v. 11). This is one of four specific reasons that God gives for His destruction of Babylon. The others are: because Nebuchadnezzar "broke the bones" of Israel (v. 17), because they contended against the Lord (v. 24), and because she has been proud against the Lord (v. 29).

This should also teach us a lesson. The judgment of God comes because of our treatment of others and our treatment of the Lord. Our love of God and love of our neighbor are inseparable.

THE SECOND PROPHECY AGAINST BABYLON

Read Jeremiah 51.

According to this prophecy, who will the Lord use to judge Babylon? How does that compare with statements made in the last prophecy? (vv. 11, 27, 28)

What is the key thought in verses 15–19? What idea would this parallel in the prophecy of chapter 50?

In verses 20–23 who is the entity referred to as "you"?

If God used Babylon as His tool to judge the nations (vv. 20–23), why does He then judge Babylon?

In verse 34, who is speaking?

In verses 45 through 48 is the reference to Babylon speaking of the city, the country, or the world-system? Why do you think so?

The point of this prophecy is that Babylon, whom God used to punish the nations, will itself be punished. We must recognize that God, who uses the wrath of man to praise Him, is just in judging those whom He uses for His purposes. For God judges a nation—or a person—based on their sin.

Within this chapter is one of the great contrasts between the true God and false gods. Idols are shameful and "a work of errors." The dull-hearted and stupid follow the carved image. But rather than *being made* by a metalsmith, God is the Maker. He has stretched out the heavens and established the earth, and He controls all the workings of nature.

A shift takes place in verses 34 and 35. The prophet has been speaking of the city or nation, but he is now shifting to speak of the world-system opposed to God as Babylon. In verses 45 through 48 especially it seems that God is calling His people of all times and places to come away from the world-system and flee the judgment of God which is coming upon the world-system. Verse 45 is strongly paralleled in Revelation 18:4, and verse 48 is echoed in Revelation 18:20. So we see that the Lord is speaking on several different levels at once. The nation of Babylonia was to be judged and overthrown. But the Lord wants us to know that the judgment of "this present evil age" (Gal. 1:4) is coming, and we need to separate ourselves from anything which would connect us with the plagues which are coming upon the world in these last days.

JUDGMENT AGAINST OTHER LANDS

In addition to judgment on Egypt and Babylon, Jeremiah gave prophecies concerning the judgment of other lands surrounding Israel. In this section we will examine Jeremiah 47 through 49 to see what we can learn from these judgment prophecies. As you read through these chapters consider similarities and differences between them. In addition, think about what we have already studied which sounds similar, and keep in mind who God is using to bring judgment on these nations.

What nations does Jeremiah prophesy against in chapters 47 through 49?

Compare Jeremiah 47:2 with Jeremiah 46:8. What similarities do you find? What is the most significant difference?

Find several examples where cities are mentioned in these passages. Why do you think Jeremiah names particular cities in these prophecies?

Reread Jeremiah 25:27–29. In these prophecies of chapters 47—49, where do you find echoes of this earlier passage?

What do these verses have in common: Jeremiah 48:44; 49:5, 8, 32, 37? What is the key idea emphasized in those verses?

Where do you find references to the Babylonians in these prophecies? (47:2; 49:30) What does that tell you?

To which countries does God give the promise that He will bring back the captives? What does this show us? (48:47; 49:6, 39)

In these chapters Jeremiah prophesies against eight different nations: Philistia, Moab, Ammon, Edom, Damascus, Kedar, Hazor, and Elam.

 KINGDOM EXTRA

Bible Atlases and Dictionaries

A good Bible atlas and Bible dictionary are valuable resources when studying biblical passages which refer to other lands. An atlas will show you where the nations are with reference to Israel and each other, and it will provide information about the physical geography, types of land, and climate of the nations being studied. A Bible dictionary will provide articles on particular lands and will frequently have articles about cities as well. The dictionary will provide background information on the history, religion, and customs of the lands which will make the passage being studied more meaningful.

Nelson's New Illustrated Bible Dictionary is an excellent one-volume dictionary for preachers, Sunday school teachers, or laypeople who are interested in getting more from their Bible study.

In these prophecies Jeremiah says that destruction is coming upon these lands. In the upheaval which accompanied the downfall of Assyria and the rise of Babylon, all the nations throughout the Middle East were shaken, and war passed through many lands.

Throughout these prophecies we see the repeated emphasis that the Lord is bringing about judgment and He is in control. The "waters risen in the north" are mentioned in the word against Philistia, and Nebuchadnezzar is named in the prophecy against Kedar and Hazor, but other than that the Babylonians are not mentioned in these prophecies even though they were to be the major source of the Lord's punishment of these nations. Rather, Jeremiah is constantly emphasizing that God is in control.

In this we need to see an expression of God's faithfulness. He is faithful to uphold his righteous rulership of the earth, He is faithful to bring righteous judgment, and He is faithful to fulfill His righteous word. But also in the midst of these words of judgment, we need to see that God is also faithfully merciful. He acts with grace and mercy as well as with judgment. After several of the prophecies God promises that He will bring back the captives. This shows us God's mercy and illustrates the fact that God will not give up on anyone. Although His judgment will always come—indeed He **must** judge evil—He is also always showing us His steadfast love.

    ### FAITH ALIVE

Prophecies of judgment are not always the most pleasant things to study. To read of war, and calamity, and terror makes us uncomfortable even though we live in a prosperous and powerful country. Yet we must see that nations such as Egypt and Babylon were the superpowers of their day—we do well to not be too secure in the political or military might of our homeland.

There are two reasons we do well not to trust in the power of our country. First, our trust needs to be in the Lord. He alone is worthy of unreserved trust. Second, we must remember that we have no homeland here. We are pilgrims who are looking forward to a homeland which God will establish. As for our country—love it, and pray for it and its leaders. Do what the Lord would call you to do to bring righteousness to your city, "for in its peace you will have peace" (Jer. 29:7).

We have seen in this lesson that God is faithful to judge, and He is also faithful to "bring back the captives"—He is faithful in His mercy. As a final meditation on the faithfulness of God, consider Exodus 34:5–7. In this passage the Lord is proclaiming His name. Take some time to think about what the Lord proclaims and how His words relate to what we have studied in regard to God's faithfulness in judgment and mercy. Write some of your thoughts in the space below.

Lesson 6/Hope for the Future
(Jeremiah 30—33)

Throughout our study of the Book of Jeremiah we have primarily seen the faithfulness of God expressed as His just judgment against the wicked. Yet within the Book of Jeremiah is one of the most hopeful and most important segments of prophecy which concern the future of the nation of Israel. It is called "The Book of Consolation" because the Lord specifically told Jeremiah to write it for the people who would see these things fulfilled. Because the Book of Consolation deals with prophecy about the restoration of Israel and the latter days, it has stirred up much interest and has been subjected to widely different interpretations. As we study these chapters, we will focus more on what the Lord wants to tell us about ourselves right now rather than on what we might be able to fit into our prophetic scheme of choice.

THE PROMISE OF RETURN

Read Jeremiah 30.

Why does the Lord tell Jeremiah to write a book? (v. 3)

What is the time of Jacob's trouble? (v. 7)

What will happen when Jacob is saved out of his trouble? (vv. 8, 9)

Who will the people of Israel serve at that time? (v. 9) Who is this referring to?

In verses 10 and 11 the Lord says that He will save Israel. What is the primary manifestation this salvation takes in the verses?

The Lord speaks of Israel as being wounded and forsaken in verses 12 through 15. Who has wounded Israel? Why?

However, verses 16 and 17 indicate a reversal of fortunes. What expressions does the prophet use to show this? Why will this occur?

Verses 18 through 24 give a word which is characteristic of oracles concerning the day of the Lord: there is a promise of blessing and prominence to the faithful of Israel, and there is the promise of God's wrath being visited upon the enemies of the Lord. What statements in that section refer to Israel being blessed with land? What statements refer to them being blessed with fertility? What verse is messianic?

Upon whom will the anger and fury of the Lord fall? (v. 23) When will these things take place? (v. 24)

This chapter opens with the command to Jeremiah to write a book. The Lord tells Jeremiah to write a book *because* He will bring the people back from captivity. This deliverance means they would be free from the enslavement to foreign powers. Their bondage will be broken, and they will be free to serve the

Lord and to serve "David their king" (a clear messianic reference). This salvation is manifested in us who have turned to the Lord Jesus Christ. We were enslaved by a foreigner (the devil), and the yoke of sin has been broken off our necks. We have now been freed to serve God and our King, Jesus.

Although the Lord promises Israel a return to their land, He also says that correction and punishment *will* occur. Israel will be wounded and afflicted by enemies, and the Lord will allow it because of their sins. Yet there will be a reversal of fortunes and "those who devour you shall be devoured," and "those who plunder you shall become plunder" (v. 16).

The Lord goes on to promise restoration to their land (v. 18), restoration of worship (v. 19), restoration of the blessings of family and plenty (vv. 19, 20), and restoration of rulership (v. 21). The promise of restoration to the land uses language which shows both rural (tents) and urban (city) elements. This shows that full and complete restoration will take place.

THE RESTORATION OF ISRAEL AND JUDAH

Read Jeremiah 31 and answer the following questions.

What verse from chapter 30 is similar to 31:1? What does this tell you?

How does God describe His love? (v. 3) What are the results of His love as shown to Israel? (v. 4)

What are some of the indications that this prophecy is for all of Israel, not just the northern or southern kingdom?

As the remnant returns to the land, how is their emotional or mental state described? (v. 9) What will it be like when they are back in the land? (vv. 12–14)

Where is Ramah? What is significant about Ramah? (See Jer. 40:1) Do verses 15–17 refer to Israel or to Judah?

Does Jeremiah 31:18–20 refer to Israel or Judah? Does Jeremiah 31:23–26 refer to Israel or Judah?

What is the promise contained in verses 23–26?

Compare verse 28 with Jeremiah 1:10. Comment on the parallels.

In the context of the Book of Jeremiah, explain the saying in verse 29. What is the Lord's response?

Verses 31 to 34 speak of a new covenant. How has the Lord fulfilled this?

What is the message of verses 35–37? How should this affect our interpretation of this chapter?

What is promised in verses 38 to 40? How would you apply this promise personally?

In chapter 31 God is passing from speaking just about the restoration of their fortunes and land to speaking about the restoration of relationship. He speaks of grace and love that He will give to Israel, and His love is everlasting. God loved us before we were born, and His love for us is the motivating factor in His plan of salvation. **That's** an everlasting love!

Because of His love God will rebuild Israel, and He will bring them joy and plenty. But also note that God speaks of a reunifying of Israel and Judah. The breach between Israel and Judah will be healed.

The Lord says to sing with gladness, for He will gather the remnant of Israel and bring them back to the land, where they will rejoice and sing (vv. 12, 13).

The passage beginning with verse 27 tells us of a new relationship which God will establish with His people. Verse 28 would have had a special meaning to Jeremiah because the Lord uses the same terminology which He used in calling Jeremiah. It is as though God is saying, "I gave you an assignment, and now you can see how you have fit into my plan." It may not always be clear how your work fits into the big picture of what God is doing, but if you are faithful to be obedient, God will see to it that your work bears fruit.

The Lord then refers to a proverb, "The fathers have eaten sour grapes, and the children's teeth are set on edge" (v. 29). This expression meant that the children suffered for their father's sins (see Lam. 5:7). However, the statement was taken as an excuse—as an escape from responsibility. The people said that the judgment they were facing was a result of their father's sins, as though their own sin had nothing to do with it. So the Lord corrects their understanding by telling them that each individual will bear his own sin.

Then God promises a new day in which every person will know the Lord, and the covenant relationship which the Lord will have with His people will be a matter of the heart. The complete fulfillment of this prophecy awaits the coming of the Lord and the fulfillment of His kingdom (Rev. 21:3); however, we experience this blessing in part through the work of Jesus Christ and the abiding presence of the Holy Spirit.

In verses 35 to 37, God promised Israel that they will always be a people, and He will not cast them away. Some interpreters emphasize that the church is a continuation of the work God began with Israel, while others stress the discontinuity between Israel and the church. Both perspectives are true: The church is a continuation of the work of God, yet God still has a program for Israel.

Verses 38–40 promise that Jerusalem would be rebuilt and expanded, and the area where the dead bodies were stacked would be holy to the Lord. This has a beautiful application to us. As the Lord brings us back from captivity and restores us, He will also restore those parts of our lives which were full of death. He will make them holy and they will be set apart for the Lord's purposes.

THE SIGN OF THE PURCHASED FIELD

Read Jeremiah 32.

Where was Jeremiah when he received this word from the Lord? (v. 2) Why was he there? (vv. 3–5)

What event did the Lord use to speak to Jeremiah? (vv. 6–8)

What was the word the Lord gave to Jeremiah related to buying the field? (vv. 13–15)

What did Jeremiah do after giving the word of the Lord? (v. 16)

How does Jeremiah begin his prayer? To what characteristics or attributes of God does Jeremiah allude in his prayer? (vv. 17–22)

To what parts of the history of God's dealing with mankind does Jeremiah allude? (vv. 20–22) Why is it important that this history is mentioned?

What is Jeremiah's request or question in this prayer? (vv. 24, 25)

To which of His attributes does God refer in His response to Jeremiah? (v. 27)

What does God say He will do to the city? Why? (vv. 28–35)

What specific sins of the people of Judah does the Lord mention in His response to Jeremiah? (vv. 28–35)

Go through verses 37–41 and list every "I will . . ." the Lord says.

What is God's final answer to Jeremiah's question? (vv. 42–44)

While Jerusalem was under siege, Jeremiah was imprisoned in the city. Jeremiah's cousin visited him and asked him to buy his field in Jeremiah's hometown. Then Jeremiah knew that the Lord had spoken to him.

Jeremiah bought the field, proclaiming this as a sign that the time would come when property was again possessed in the land. Then Jeremiah prayed, saying basically, "You say that fields will again be possessed, but at the same time You have told me that the city will fall! What's going on here?"

In answer to Jeremiah, the Lord begins by reminding him that He is omnipotent—God is all-powerful and He can accomplish His word. Then God says that, yes, He will give the city into the hands of the Chaldeans because of all the evil which the people have done. He mentions specifically that they defiled the temple of the Lord with their idols, and they built the high places and sacrificed their children. Therefore, the city will be destroyed and the people will be punished.

Yet when their punishment is over, the Lord will bring them back to the land and will restore them. The Lord emphasizes that He will be the One who restores their fortunes by repeating "I will . . ." nine times in verses 36–41 (including one "I will not . . .").

- I will gather them

- I will bring them back
- I will be their God
- I will give them one heart
- I will make an everlasting covenant
- I will not turn away from doing them good
- I will put My fear in their hearts
- I will rejoice over them
- I will assuredly plant them in this land.

The Lord is very thorough in His redemption, and when He brings restoration, He heals everything that was broken. Our redemption is no less thorough, for God has given us salvation, sonship, and a secure future in the kingdom of heaven, along with the blessings of abiding in the true Vine, who is Christ (John 15:1–8).

God's final answer to Jeremiah must be placed in the setting of His first words. There is nothing too hard for the Lord; therefore, He will destroy the city, yet He will also bring back the captives. The Lord will always fulfill His word, and though we may not see how the Lord can do what He has promised, we can rest in the security of His word.

THE RESTORATION OF JERUSALEM

Read Jeremiah 33.

When did this prophecy come to Jeremiah? (v. 1)

In verse 2, what is "it"?

When the Lord says "Call to Me . . ." (v. 3) what is He saying? Is He asking for our requests?

What is the primary promise in verses 4–9? What other promises are given? How do they relate to the primary promise?

The Lord speaks of the return of people to the once-desolate city of Jerusalem in verses 10–13. Why are shepherds particularly singled out? (vv. 12, 13)

Who is the Branch of righteousness? (v. 15)

Who will be called "THE LORD OUR RIGHTEOUS-NESS"? (v. 16)

In this segment of the prophecy the house of David is promised continuity. What other group is also promised continuity? (v. 21)

There are many parallels between verses 19–22 and 31:35–37. What are some of the differences?

What is the purpose of verses 23–26?

Jeremiah received this word after the events of chapter 32. Jeremiah was still in prison, and he probably needed encouragement as he sat, isolated and confined, waiting while the siege dragged on and the famine in the city worsened. So it is in the midst of a desperate situation that the Lord comes to him and tells him that he will see great things beyond what he knows.

First, the Lord said that He made, formed, and established "it," yet He does not say what "it" is. But the Lord knows of what He speaks. "It" is whatever God decides; God will determine and bring to pass *anything* that He chooses.

Second, the Lord says to call upon Him and He will show us great things which we know not. The two key words in this verse are "call" and "know."

WORD WEALTH

Call, *qara'* (kah-*rah*); To call out to someone; cry out; to address someone; to shout, or speak out, to proclaim. *Qara'* often describes calling out loudly in an attempt to get someone's attention (Is. 58:1), or for calling upon the Lord or upon His name. (See Is. 55:6; Joel 2:32.) Sometimes *qara'* means "to name something," that is, to call it by its name. Similarly, *qara'* involves the naming of places, holidays, or children. *Qara'* appears more than 700 times in the Bible.[1]

WORD WEALTH

Know, *yada'* (yah-*dah*); To know, to perceive, to distinguish, to recognize, to acknowledge, to be aquainted with; to recognize, esteem, and endorse. When Scripture speaks of God's making known His name, it refers to His revealing (through deeds or events) what His name truly means.[2]

With this information about these words, we can now determine what the Lord is saying with this statement. The Lord did not say, "Request of Me . . ."; He said, "Call to Me." God is asking that we call out to Him in earnestness and dependence.

The Lord goes on to tell Jeremiah some of the great things He will do. The Lord promises that the city of Jerusalem will be rebuilt, but more specifically He is promising that the places that were torn down in order to fortify the walls against attack would be restored.

This section contains a great promise for us, because we all have places in our lives which have been "torn down." Our self-fortification is futile, but He will see to it that those parts of us which were destroyed will be rebuilt.

As Jeremiah continues this word about the restoration of Jerusalem he says that the city, which was desolate, will again be inhabited, and people will praise the Lord. The house of David (represented by Jesus Christ) is told that the rulership will not pass from him, and the priests and Levites are also told that they will have a perpetual office of worship.

The Lord closes this prophecy with a correction. The people were saying, "The Lord chose two families and the Lord has also cast them away." But God says that although it may look bleak at the moment, He has made promises to Jacob and to David, and His promises are surer than the sunrise.

 FAITH ALIVE

In this lesson we have seen that God has a plan for Israel, yet *we* are not excluded from those promises. One may wonder how this can be so. The answer is in Jesus Christ. He came to be Israel's Messiah, and also the Gentiles' hope.

Through Jesus we can participate in God's promises to Israel because Jesus was a descendant of Israel, and we are *in Christ!* In this way, God has made us partakers of His promises, and Jesus has broken down the wall that separated Jew and Gentile—we become one in Christ (Eph. 2:11–18).

Look up the following verses and explain what they tell us about God's promises.
Romans 15:8–13

2 Corinthians 1:19, 20

2 Peter 1:2–4

1. *Spirit-Filled Life® Bible* (Nashville: Thomas Nelson Publishers, 1991), 1107–1108, "Word Wealth: Jer. 33:3, call."
2. Ibid., 87, "Word Wealth: Ex. 3:7, know."

Among the Ashes, Hope
(Lamentations)

The Lamentations of Jeremiah were written shortly after the fall of Jerusalem. These five poems vividly portray, in the thought parallelism of Hebrew poetry, the final desperate days of the siege of Jerusalem and the humiliation of the captives after the city has fallen. The picture of defeat is stark and depressing. The judgment of God has been poured out on Jerusalem because of her sins.

Yet even in his contemplation of judgment and destruction, Jeremiah retains hope. He knows that God is merciful and loving: His mercies are new every morning; His faithfulness is great.

Lesson 7/The Severity of Faithfulness
(Lamentations 1—5)

Have you ever seen a ghost town? You wonder what happened which led to the demise of the town. Where did the people go? It is disconcerting to see a place which was once so full of life now dead.

Jerusalem was like that—destroyed and broken beyond all hope of recovery. Jeremiah saw the destruction of Jerusalem with his own eyes, and he expressed the wrenching emotion he felt in five poems which make up the Book of Lamentations.

The poems of Lamentations (with the exception of the last) are acrostic, each verse beginning with a successive letter of the Hebrew alphabet. Working successfully within this framework makes these poems one of the masterpieces of Hebrew poetry. The last poem is a prayer, and as the prophet poured out his heart to God he did not constrain himself to the acrostic pattern. The author of this work is not named, but ancient scholars and most modern scholars have attributed it to Jeremiah.

THE FIRST POEM

Read Lamentations 1.
What is the overall theme of Lamentations 1?

What is the reason for the desolation of Jerusalem? (vv. 5, 8, 18)

In verse 12 Jeremiah shifts from third person (she, her) to first person (I, me). Does this indicate that Jeremiah is now speaking of himself? If not, who is speaking?

Jeremiah ends this poem with a prayer. In which verse does the prayer begin?

The prayer is in the first person. Is Jeremiah praying himself or is he speaking for another?

What is the main request of the prayer? (vv. 21, 22)

In this first poem, Jeremiah is focusing on the condition of Jerusalem. He uses many figures of speech to show how Jerusalem has fallen. He likens Jerusalem to a princess and says that this princess has become like a widow and a slave. Her lovers do not comfort her, her friends have become her enemies, and her enemies have become her masters. The reason for all this tragedy is the unfaithfulness of Jerusalem. The city had turned away from the Lord and had forgotten the high purpose which the Lord had for her.

FAITH ALIVE

One of the most significant statements in Lamentations 1:9: "She did not consider her destiny; therefore her collapse was awesome." This verse is speaking of the fact that the people of Jerusalem did not consider that the Lord had chosen them, but they had followed other gods. Therefore, the judgment of the Lord came upon them.

This is a call for each of us to recognize the great destiny that God has in store for us. We were created in God's image, and we have been redeemed by God's Son. We are partakers of God's Spirit, and we must live according to God's kingdom.

Look up the following verses and summarize what they tell you about your destiny in Christ.

Ephesians 2:4-7

Hebrews 12:28

1 Corinthians 2:9

John 15:16

In the midst of his mourning and sorrow, Jeremiah confesses that the Lord is righteous (v. 18). The sins of the people have brought this sorrow to pass, and for God to be righteous and faithful He must judge as well as bless. This is apparent by examining the meaning of the word "righteous."

 FAITH ALIVE

Righteous, *tsaddiq* (tsahd-*deek*); One who is right, just, clear, clean, righteous; a person who is characterized by fairness, integrity, and justice in his dealings. Occurring more than 200 times, *tsaddiq* is derived from the verb *tsadaq,* "to be righteous, justified, clear." *Tsadaq* and its derivatives convey justice and integrity in one's lifestyle. Being righteous brings a person light and gladness (Ps. 97:11). *Tsaddiq* occurs sixty-six times in Proverbs alone. See especially Proverbs 4:18; 18:10; 24:16. It is the *tsaddiq* who shall live by his faith in Habakkuk 2:4. Yahweh is *tsaddiq* (just and fair) at all times, even when ordaining punishments.[1]

Jeremiah ends this poem with a prayer for vindication (v. 20). But he prays not that the Lord will pardon or deliver them from their suffering; rather, his request is that the judgment of the Lord will fall also upon the enemies of Jerusalem. He is making the example of Jerusalem universal. The judgment being visited upon Judah is also deserved by **all** other nations and **every** individual.

THE SECOND POEM

Read Lamentations 2.

What is the theme of Lamentations 2?

The first section of this poem covers verses 1 to 10. In this section, how many references are there to the Lord doing something?

What is the "footstool" referred to in verse 1?

In verses 6 through 10 what references are made to the leadership of the nation?

What verses refer to the temple being destroyed? Which verses deal with the destruction of the city? (vv. 6–9)

In verses 11 through 17 who is the one speaking to Jerusalem?

What does Jeremiah say about the false prophets? (v. 14) What did the prophets fail to do?

Several verses throughout the chapter refer to the young children (vv. 11, 12, 19, 20). What is said about them? Cite the verse.

Chapter two also ends with a prayer. In what verse does the prayer begin and what is the theme of the prayer?

Even in the destruction of the city, Jeremiah sees that God is faithful. God is in control of the real enemies (v. 3), He is the ultimate source of this judgment (v. 8), and He is being faithful to His commandment (v. 17).

Jeremiah cries out for his city and his people, and he especially laments for the children. He says that the children faint in the streets (v. 11), they ask for food and die in their mothers' arms (v. 12). The ruin of Zion is as great as an ocean, and there is no one to heal her.

Verse 19 asks the people to pray and again the children are mentioned as a reason to pray. The prophet asks the Lord to consider the misery which the judgment has brought about, and he wonders if the mercy of the Lord has failed. Yet even as he is reaching the depths of despair, we are coming to the turning point where Jeremiah makes some of the greatest statements about the mercy of God found in all of Scripture.

THE THIRD POEM

This poem is the longest of the five. It marks a turning point in the development of Jeremiah's thought about this tragedy.

Read chapter 3 and answer the following questions. What is the theme of chapter 3?

Notice that Jeremiah initially refers to the Lord as He. When does he first mention the Lord by name?

After shifting from "He" to "the Lord" Jeremiah still uses the third person. When does Jeremiah shift to the second person (You)?

This poem contains two sections of complaint followed by sections of hope. Fill in the outline below to specify the location of these divisions.

THEME

I. First complaint: verses 1– _____

II. First section of hope: verses _____ – _____

III. Second complaint: verses _____ – _____

IV. Second section of hope: verses _____ – _____

What are some of the reasons that we can hope in the Lord? (vv. 19–42, 55–66)

What three things are mentioned of which the Lord does not approve? (vv. 34–36)

In view of the Lord's mercies, what ought we to do? (vv. 26–30, 40, 41)

In making the transition into the second complaint, what does Jeremiah state is the cause of the anger of God coming upon them? (v. 42)

What action on Jeremiah's part brings us into the second section of hope? (v. 55)

In the second section of hope, what does the writer say God has done for him? (vv. 55–66)

In verse 21 Jeremiah turns a corner in his thinking. In spite of the affliction, and in spite of the difficulties he sees, Jeremiah remembers that the Lord is merciful and faithful. He remembers that the sins of the people make them deserving of total destruction, and it is only the mercy of God which saves them from annihilation. Therefore, there *is* hope in the Lord. Even though the Lord may punish, we can hope for His salvation.

Jeremiah is now using the second person: he has switched from complaining *about* what God has done to complaining *to* God. The Lord is no longer that external, distant oppressor, He is near—Jeremiah can talk to Him. Helmut Thielicke says that we must recognize that God has spoken to us and that He expects a reply. Thus, the essence of good theology is dialogue with God.[2]

Things are so hard and God seems so distant at times that we feel our prayers don't get past the ceiling. In times like this we need to do what Jeremiah did: call to mind the mercies of God and recall who God is and what He is really like. "The Lord is gracious and full of compassion, slow to anger and great in mercy. The Lord is good to all, and His tender mercies are over all His works" (Ps. 145:8, 9).

This brings us to Jeremiah's prayer—even more significantly, to the fact that Jeremiah is now confident that the Lord is near and He will hear his prayer (vv. 55–57). What Jeremiah requests is actually a fulfillment of judgment. He asks that judgment come to completion because he knows that the completion of judgment will bring deliverance to the righteous and a vindication of their suffering. Therefore, we also look for the completion of the judgment of God. This poem teaches us to live in repentant preparation for the completion of God's judgment, and also to live in expectation of the completion of His judgment. The completion of God's judgment will bring the fullness of the rulership of God to the earth, which will mean nothing less than the coming of His kingdom.

THE FOURTH POEM

Read Lamentations 4 and answer these questions.

Consider verses 1 and 2. To what is verse 1 referring when it speaks of the gold and precious stones?

Notice how speaking of the judgment progresses throughout the chapter from the infants to the adults to the rulers. What verses refer to each of these classes of people? (vv. 4–8)

In which verses does the prophet admit the sins of the people? (vv. 13, 14) What sins are named?

What incredible event is spoken of in verse 12? Why did that event happen?

Compare verse 15 with Leviticus 13:45 and Deuteronomy 28:65. In light of these verses, comment on the meaning of verse 15.

What is the main idea behind verse 17? In whom does it suggest the people were trusting?

How does Jeremiah express the complete subjugation of the people to the Babylonians in verses 18 to 20? What progression in the domination of Babylon is shown?

What nation is mentioned in verses 20 and 21? Why? (See Obadiah.) What is the message of verses 21 and 22?

In this poem Jeremiah returns to consider the condition of Jerusalem and the people in particular. The young are starving, the wealthy are living in the ash heaps, and the rulers have so changed in appearance due to prolonged want that they are not even recognized in the streets.

The sins of the nation have brought them to this state, and although the punishment is great, the prophet admits that it is deserved. The punishment of their sin was greater than that of Sodom (v. 6), and the rulers sinned and shed innocent blood in the city (v. 13). This punishment is from the hand of the Lord (v. 11).

The false prophets and priests must shoulder a major part of the blame for this calamity (v. 13). They are now treated like lepers by their own people, and they are not wanted anywhere (v. 15).

Jeremiah also reflects back to the last days of the siege. The people still vainly hoped for help from Egypt; they still were trusting in man rather than in God. But the inevitable end came: the people were tracked down in the streets of the city, and those who escaped were unable to flee. Their very lives ("The breath of our nostrils") were trapped, and they were made captives to the Babylonians.

The poem ends with the hope that the enemies of Judah with be judged, now that Zion's punishment has been completed.

THE FIFTH POEM

Read Lamentations 5 and answer these questions.

With whom does Jeremiah compare the people? (v. 3) What is significant about that comparison?

Why did the people have to pay for water and wood? (v. 4) What does this tell us about the condition of the people?

Verses 10–13 tell what happened when Jerusalem fell. List the incidents and indignities which the people suffered.

A loss of rulership and joy are indicated in verses 14 through 16. What statements are made which show the loss of these two things?

What is the cause of their predicament, and what is the answer to it? (vv. 16–22)

Comment on the closing verse of this book (v. 22). What does it tell us about Jeremiah's attitude? What can we learn from that statement?

This poem is a closing prayer, and through most of this chapter the first person plural is used (we, us). Jeremiah can finally speak for all the people and cry out to God with them—not just for them.

Jeremiah compares the people to orphans and widows. These were among the most vulnerable and powerless people in the ancient world, so the prophet is declaring that they have lost everything. Having no possessions, they must now pay for the bare necessities of survival. They must labor constantly to meet their basic needs.

Faced with this complete loss and total defeat the people can only turn to the One who cannot be lost or overcome. The Lord is steadfast and changeless; He alone can be depended upon when everything around you is shaken. So the people cry out to God, "Turn us back to You" (v. 21). There is a recognition here that God's grace and mercy are the source of everything. We live and have our being in Him (Acts 17:28), and our love for Him is due to His loving us first (1 John 4:19). The cry to "turn us back" is a recognition that God is the source of everything—even our repentance.

Yet the prayer ends on an uncertain note. Can we be certain that the Lord will receive us back? We have the promises of God to receive all those who come to Him, and to forgive and save the sinner who puts his trust in Christ. Yet we never command God to do anything. Even when our confidence is based on His Word, we must be mindful that we are totally dependent on God's mercy and grace. We ought never to presume on the mercy of God, but we should constantly live in humble dependence on His goodness.

 FAITH ALIVE

In studying this book, the theme of repentance has been pervasive. It is appropriate that it is so, for the proper response to judgment, and the response the Lord desires, is repentance. Yet one of the things we have seen is that repentance is a lifestyle, not just an act. The sins in which we have been entangled seek to snare us again and again. Repentance involves turning from sin and then continuing to turn from sin. This is the repentance Jesus called for repeatedly when He said, "Go, and sin no more."

Look up the following verses and comment on what they tell you about repentance being a process.

Acts 26:20

Galatians 5:1

Revelation 2:5

1. *Spirit-Filled Life® Bible* (Nashville: Thomas Nelson Publishers, 1991), 1145, "Word Wealth: Lam. 1:18, righteous."

2. Helmut Thielicke, *A Little Exercise for Young Theologians* (Grand Rapids: William B. Eerdmans Publishing Co., 1962), 34–35.

Best of Times, Worst of Times
(Ezekiel)

Charles Dickens used these phrases in the opening of his *Tale of Two Cities,* a story about happenings in London and Paris during the French Revolution. They also could apply to the Book of Ezekiel. As in Dickens' classic, the action centers in two cities embroiled in turmoil and tragedy. Both books even end with an escape from the conflict to the relative safety of a new home. In Ezekiel, however, that final escape only comes about in the prophesied future.

Though somewhat younger than Jeremiah, Ezekiel shared with him the experience of living through one of the most tragic eras of Israel's history. Also like Jeremiah, Ezekiel did not live to see the fulfillment of the promises God had prophesied through his words. Ezekiel, too, finds mercy contained within God's judgments. With God, all things are possible— even the restoration of Israel.

Lesson 8/Experiencing God's Faithfulness in Exile
(Ezekiel 1—3; 33:1–20)

"Exile" conjures up many images: a wandering pilgrim or a group of political leaders setting up a governmental structure to organize resistance to an oppressive conqueror. The images may be courageous, melancholy, hopeful, or lonely. But one common element in all the images is a sense of homesickness—the yearning to get back to the place where you belong. That feeling is evident in Psalm 137 which was written during the Babylonian exile:

> By the rivers of Babylon,
> There we sat down, yea, we wept
> When we remembered Zion.
> We hung our harps
> Upon the willows in the midst of it.
> For there those who carried us away
>   captive asked of us a song,
> And they who plundered us
>   requested mirth,
> Saying, "Sing us one of the songs
>   of Zion!"
> How shall we sing the LORD's song
> In a foreign land?
> Psalm 137:1–4

Exile implies a yearning for something without which life is incomplete. In this lesson we will look at the life of one of these exiles: Ezekiel. He was not just an exile on this earth, but he was also an exile from his own country. He was one of those Jews who sat down by the rivers of Babylon—in his case, the River Chebar. Through his life and his message we can learn how the Lord is faithful to us in exile.

EZEKIEL'S VISION

Read Ezekiel chapter 1.

When did these visions come to Ezekiel? (v. 1) What was happening in Jerusalem and in the ancient world?

In verse 1 what does the reference to the thirtieth year signify?

What was Ezekiel's occupation? (v. 3)

Compare the living creatures which Ezekiel saw with the living creatures which John saw in Revelation 4:6–8. What similarities and differences do you find? Why do you think the writers use such awkward language in their descriptions of these creatures?

What is the significance of the four faces of the living creatures? (v. 10)

Compare Ezekiel's vision of the throne in verses 26 through 28 with Revelation 4:2–5.

The Book of Ezekiel begins in the fifth year of the captivity of King Jehoiachin, which would have been about 593 B.C. Ezekiel makes reference to the thirtieth year. The most probable explanation is that Ezekiel was thirty years old when he began his prophetic ministry. This tells us that Jeremiah began his ministry about three years *before* Ezekiel was born. Therefore, Ezekiel had grown up hearing Jeremiah's prophecies, and he was now an exile in Babylon as Jeremiah had foretold.

Ezekiel had a series of visions from God. The first vision contains strange, indescribable creatures and the brightness of the glory of God. These creatures are the cherubim, great angelic beings which surround the throne of God.

 BEHIND THE SCENES

The Cherubim. Cherubim are the created beings assigned to guard the throne of God (Ps. 99:1) as well as the ark of the covenant and the mercy seat (Ex. 25:18–22; 37:7–9). Cherubim (plural for cherub) guarded the Tree of Life to keep man from eating of it and, therefore, living forever in his sins. Thus more than one angel guarded the entrance to Eden. The fullest description of cherubim is in Ezekiel 10, where they are closely related to the glory of God and have a part in its presence and its withdrawal, moving at the Almighty's direction.[1]

Ezekiel's description of these creatures is difficult to follow and hard to imagine. He is attempting to describe something which is outside of human experience. He was seeing in the spirit and beholding things outside of the normal constraints of space and time, yet his descriptions are constrained by human language, which is limited by space and time.

Ezekiel also saw the throne of God and his vision has much in common with John's vision of the throne in the Book of Revelation. They both describe the throne as being like precious stones, and they both say that there was a rainbow around the throne. The combination of similarities leads to the obvious conclusion that both Ezekiel and John saw the throne of God as it truly exists in the spirit, and they beheld the glory of God.

The subject of the glory of God could fill a book in itself. The fall of man included the loss of the glory of God which abode with man. The worship of God in both the Old and New Testaments includes the return of God's glory. And the promise of God is that one day the glory of the Lord will be revealed to all flesh. The point we need to see is that God's glory comes with His call. We may not always have a dramatic vision like Ezekiel or John did, but when the Lord calls us to do His work, He brings His glory to that work to give it weight and substance.

EZEKIEL'S CALL

Read Ezekiel 2:1—3:3.

Who gave Ezekiel the strength to stand before the Lord? (2:2)

What adjectives does the Lord use to describe the children of Israel? (2:4, 5) List them and define them.

What does verse 5 imply about the willingness of Israel to hear the word that the Lord is giving Ezekiel?

What three things does the Lord tell Ezekiel not to be afraid of? (2:6)

What does God command Ezekiel to do? (2:7)

What was on the scroll that God gave to Ezekiel? (2:10)

What does the scroll represent?

What does God command in 3:3? What is the reason for this command?

What is the meaning or significance of the taste of the scroll? (3:3)

When Ezekiel saw the glory of God, he fell on his face. Throughout Scripture this is a common response to seeing the glory of God. He was called to be God's spokesman to a nation which was rebellious and stubborn.

God then says to Ezekiel, "Don't be rebellious like they are" (v. 8). And He asks Ezekiel to take and eat what God gives him. It is in this act that God is calling Ezekiel, for what God is giving him to eat is the message which the Lord has for him to take to the children of Israel in exile. This message is not a pleasant message but is a message of "lamentations and mourning and woe." Yet when Ezekiel eats it, it is sweet as honey to his taste.

Whenever we receive God's word, there is a sweetness which we experience, for God's words always contain hope. As we saw in Jeremiah, and as we will see in Ezekiel, God's judgment does come upon the rebellious, but His judgment also holds promise for the penitent.

EZEKIEL'S MISSION

Read Ezekiel 3:4–15 and 3:22–27.

What is Ezekiel to speak to the house of Israel? (3:4)

Why is the lack of a language barrier emphasized in verses 4–7? Who might the Lord be referring to as "a people of unfamiliar speech"? (v. 5) To what might the "many people of unfamiliar speech" (v. 6) refer?

Why will Israel not hear the word which Ezekiel brings? (3:7)

Look through chapters 2 and 3. How many times does the Lord call the children of Israel "rebellious"?

The expression which is translated "impudent" in verse 7 literally means "strong of forehead." How does this help you better appreciate what God tells Ezekiel in verses 8 and 9?

In verse 10 God again tells Ezekiel to receive His words. How is this command different from the command for Ezekiel to receive God's words in 2:7—3:3? What does this difference in emphasis mean?

In your own words describe Ezekiel's emotional and mental state after this vision (3:15).

In Ezekiel 3:22–24, Ezekiel again sees a vision of the glory of the throne of God. Does he go to the same place where he saw the first vision? Why?

What does God tell Ezekiel to do? (3:24)

What does God tell Ezekiel the people will do to him? (3:25)

What does God tell Ezekiel He will do to him? (3:26, 27)

Ezekiel has been called by God, and is given the commission to go to the house of Israel and, as God said, "Speak with My words to them." This emphasis on speaking only what God wanted him to speak is prominent in Ezekiel's call. The Lord goes on to say that Israel will not listen to His words even though there is no language barrier. They are in a strange land, governed by foreigners, and there were probably captives from other lands living in villages near them. And God says, "Your foreign rulers would hear My words, and these many other people of unfamiliar speech would listen, but Israel will not listen."

The reason Israel will not hear God's word is because they are hard-hearted, impudent, and rebellious. In these two chapters the Lord calls the house of Israel "rebellious" eight times, and in Ezekiel 3:7 the expression "strong of forehead" is used of the people. But God tells Ezekiel that He will make Ezekiel's forehead stronger than theirs!

God again tells Ezekiel to receive His words, but this time He tells Ezekiel to receive them into his heart rather than into his stomach. God is telling Ezekiel that He wants him to know and understand what God is saying, and not just to regurgitate what he had received.

After receiving this vision of God, Ezekiel was in a state of turmoil and disquiet. He returned to his village and remained in a state of astonishment for a week. Then the Lord told him to go out to the plain and shut himself inside his house. Finally, God says that He Himself will put constraints on Ezekiel by making him mute except when He has a word for Ezekiel to give. Ezekiel must have been a *very* unusual person to be around! He acted out messages, he did strange things, and he couldn't talk most of the time. But all of a sudden he would speak and say, "Thus saith the Lord."

EZEKIEL'S MESSAGE

In Ezekiel 3:16–21 the Lord tells Ezekiel that he will be a watchman for the house of Israel. It is his duty to give them the warnings which God gives him. This idea is expanded upon in chapter 33, so we will look at both of these passages to discover the essence of Ezekiel's message.

Read Ezekiel 3:16–21, and Ezekiel 33:1–20.

What is Ezekiel commanded to do as a watchman? (3:17)

What responsibility does this put on Ezekiel? What statement shows the seriousness of this responsibility? (3:18–21)

The Lord speaks to Ezekiel about warning the wicked and the righteous in 3:18–21. What difference do you see in the response of the wicked and the righteous?

In chapter 33, Israel says that there is no hope for living because their sins are upon them. In what verse is this statement made? What is God's momentous response to that statement?

What is the central message of chapter 33:12–16? State it in your own words.

What does this tell us about how we should live? How can we succeed in that kind of lifestyle? Upon whom can we depend for help?

On what basis does the Lord judge? (33:20)

As the watchman for the house of Israel, Ezekiel was to give warnings to the people; he was not responsible for their response. If Ezekiel did not give the warning, then he would be responsible for the lives that were lost. But if he gave the warning and lives were lost because people did not heed, then he was not responsible.

Rather, it was each individual who was responsible for his own life. This theme of individual responsibility is important in the Book of Ezekiel. As the nation of Judah fell into decay, the plan of God for corporate Israel fell into the background and the message of God to the individual became more prominent. Therefore, the individual is given the opportunity to turn to God or away from God.

God continues in 33:12–16 to emphasize the actions and choices of the individual. A person's day-to-day choices have a great bearing on his or her destiny. You cannot "save up" righteousness in order to have a reserve to fall back on when you sin. This is what Jesus meant by the parable of the unprofitable servants (Luke 17:7–10)—even when we have done everything right we have nothing to boast of.

But on the other hand, God readily accepts the repentance of the wicked. If one cannot "save up" righteousness, neither does one need to earn his way out of sin. The parable of the prodigal son shows us how willing—indeed, how expectant God is for the return of the sinner, and for His full acceptance (Luke 15:11–32).

 FAITH ALIVE

Through this chapter we have seen in God's call to Ezekiel a call and a promise to each of us. Like Ezekiel, you may be at a point in your life where it seems that the promise of ministry which you were moving toward has crumbled. But God wants you to see *Him!* And He wants you to know that

His plans for you are never derailed by external factors, even if they seem to loom large in the sight of man.

Furthermore, when God gives you an assignment, it will be sweet. This does not mean there will be no hardships, it does not mean everything will go well, it does not even mean that people will accept what the Lord is doing in and through you. But receiving and being filled with the purpose of God will bring a sweetness into your being which will endure through whatever else you face.

Finally, we are also called to be watchmen. We may not have the same call or the same level of responsibility which Ezekiel had, but we are called to be obedient to say what the Lord wants us to say. We are also called, like Ezekiel, to be silent when the Lord does not want us to say anything, and many times that is far more difficult. But in all of these things, the key thought is obedience. Living a day-by-day walk of obedience is the main thing the Lord requires, and if you strive to live wholly for God, then He will strive to make you holy for Him.

---

1. *Spirit-Filled Life*® *Bible* (Nashville: Thomas Nelson Publishers, 1991), 11, "Kingdom Dynamics: Gen. 3:4, The Cherubim."

Lesson 9/Judgment which Calls for Repentance
(Ezekiel 4—5; 8—9; 15; 17—18)

Who was the best teacher you ever had? Usually when asked that question people automatically think of one or two teachers who stand out. It may be a special enthusiasm they had for the subject they taught, or it might be a particular concern they showed toward the students. But one thing which always makes a teacher memorable is the use of dramatic teaching methods.

One such memorable teacher was Mr. Payne, a history teacher. During his lectures he would become animated, run around the room, surround himself with chairs, and jump up on his desk as he spoke of the events which have shaped our world. Students loved him because he "acted out" history.

Ezekiel was also a memorable spokesman, using illustrations and actions to communicate his message. He used poetry, drama, riddles, parables, laments, and oracles in proclaiming his message of doom. In this lesson we will look at some of the colorful methods which Ezekiel used to get his message across to the exiles.

EZEKIEL'S ACTED PROPHECIES

Read Ezekiel chapters 4 and 5.

What different actions does Ezekiel use in these chapters to portray the siege of Jerusalem?

Describe Ezekiel's first action (4:1–3).

What does the iron plate represent? (4:3)

What is Ezekiel's second action? (4:4–8)

What is the significance of the number of days? (4:5, 6)

What is the third action Ezekiel is commanded to do? (4:9–17)

To what part of the third action does Ezekiel object? Why? What does God do?

What is the fourth action? (5:1–4)

What do the various bundles of hair represent? (5:12)

Ezekiel 5:5–17 presents the statement of God's judgment which corresponds with these actions. What reasons for this judgment are given in verses 6, 7, and 11?

What five judgments are mentioned in verse 17?

Ezekiel's first act was to build a model of Jerusalem. Clay tablets were the common medium of writing in Babylonia, so Ezekiel may have actually drawn a little map of the city on the tablet. He then built a siege wall and siege works around the tablet to illustrate that the city would be besieged.

Then Ezekiel took an iron plate, which was probably a cooking utensil similar to a griddle, and set it up between himself and the model city. This was a sign that the Lord was separated from Jerusalem. Ezekiel, as the spokesman of God, represented God in this action and the plate showed that the wall of their sin had become like iron because of their hardness.

After this, Ezekiel lay on his left side for 390 days and his right side for forty days. The meaning of the periods of time represented is unclear. The total of the two punishments is 430 years, which is the time that Israel was in Egypt prior to the Exodus. Another idea is that the total represents the approximate time that Solomon's temple stood. Whatever the exact meaning of the number of days, the thrust of the prophecy was that the punishment which Israel was to bear would be lengthy.

During the period of this prophecy, Ezekiel was ordered to eat bread which was made of a mixture of grains and legumes. This bread was to be eaten by ration along with a rationed amount of water. All of these actions were to point to the shortages which the siege would bring to the city.

Ezekiel is commanded to bake his bread over human waste. This shows the compromises with cleanliness, both ceremonial and normal, the people would have to make in the desperate days of the siege. Ezekiel was appalled at this order and objected that he had never defiled himself. So the Lord graciously allowed him to use cow dung, a common fuel in that part of the world.

Finally, Ezekiel used a sword to shave his head. God told him to burn one-third of the hair, strike one-third with the sword, and scatter one-third to the wind. But he was also to take a small number and bind them in the edge of his garment. This demonstrated the fate which awaited the people of Jerusalem: They would die from famine and disease during the siege, they would fall by the sword in the war, and they would be scattered to the four winds. Yet even in this terrible judgment God would not utterly forsake Israel—a remnant would still be saved.

Ezekiel said that the sin and rebellion of the people brought this judgment upon them. God would bring famine, and wild beasts, and pestilence, and blood, and the sword against the people of Judah because of their iniquity.

EZEKIEL'S VISIONS

Read Ezekiel 8 and 9.

Where is Ezekiel taken in this vision? (8:3)

Does he see things which are actually occurring or is he seeing things which are symbolic of what is happening in Jerusalem? Why do you think so?

What is the "image of jealousy"? (8:5)

What acts of idolatry did Ezekiel witness? (8:10–16)

Who was Tammuz? Why were the women weeping? (8:14)

What is the significance of putting the branch to their nose? (8:17)

In chapter 9 upon whom was the angel in linen supposed to put a mark? (9:3, 4) Why?

Whom were the other six angels supposed to kill? (9:5, 6) Why?

Were any people spared from death?

In the vision Ezekiel is taken to the temple area in Jerusalem, where he witnesses the idols and heathen worship taking place right in the temple area! Ezekiel saw three groups of people engaged in heathen worship. These groups are representative of the leadership of Judah, the women, and the men, thus showing that *all* of Judean society was infected with idolatry.

Into this scene of abominations, the Lord calls for His angels of judgment. Six angels appear, each with a weapon, and a seventh also comes carrying a scribe's kit. The seventh angel is told to go throughout the city and mark every righteous person who is grieved by the sin in Jerusalem. The others are to follow him and kill whoever does not receive the protecting mark on their forehead. The mark the people received was the Hebrew letter *tav* which looked like an "X" or a cross.

Some of the early church fathers commented on the significance of being marked with a cross for salvation. The cross was not a form of execution until Roman times, and it was not a sign of salvation until Jesus died for us. Yet we must remember that God knew what His plan would entail well before Ezekiel wrote.

While the angels are carrying out their grim duties Ezekiel pleads for the people, yet the Lord says that the time for mercy has expired. Because the land is full of bloodshed and the city is full of sin, the Lord will not relent in His judgment. However, just because Ezekiel referred to the destruction of all the people (9:8) does not mean that everyone was slain. Throughout the Bible we see that God is able to save the righteous even as He pours out judgment upon the wicked.

PARABLES AND RIDDLES

Read Ezekiel 17.

Who is the eagle in verse 3?

Who is represented by the cedar twig? (v. 4)

What is the "seed of the land" which is planted? (v. 5)

What is the significance of the seed becoming a "spreading vine of low stature"? (v. 6)

Who is the second eagle? (v. 7)

Why did the vine spread toward the second eagle? (vv. 7, 8)

In verses 9, 10 the Lord asks questions instead of just presenting a conclusion. What effect would this have on the hearers?

How did Zedekiah rebel against Nebuchadnezzar? (v. 15)

Verse 16 mentions two kings. Who are they?

Zedekiah broke his covenant with Nebuchadnezzar, but according to verse 19 who else did he break faith with? How? What will be the result of this transgression?

What is the meaning of verses 22–24?

The Lord begins this prophecy by retelling the recent history of Judah: the eagle is Nebuchadnezzar and the twig is King Jehoiachin. Nebuchadnezzar came and removed Jehoiachin from the land and "took some of the seed of the land and planted it"; that is, he put Zedekiah on the throne in place of Jehoiachin.

The seed grew and became a low vine. This figure is indicative of the weakness of the kingdom of Judah under Zedekiah. Nebuchadnezzar desired to break the power of Judah to rebel, so when he took Jehoiachin captive he also took the political and military leadership. In addition, he took the craftsmen who formed the economic base upon which a war could be successfully waged. But in spite of the fact that the kingdom of Judah did not have adequate resources to fight the Babylonians, they still attempted to rebel. In their desire to "become a majestic vine," Judah turned toward the Pharaoh of Egypt, the second eagle in this passage.

After presenting this story, the Lord asks, "Will it thrive?" (v. 9). Rather than closing with a definite conclusion, the Lord pulls the hearers into the process. They must now think about what will happen to this rebellious vine. They are caught by the inescapable conclusion that the vine will be uprooted and left to wither.

The Lord then reveals what these images mean, and the people see that the doom of Judah has been sealed by their rebellion against Babylon. In Babylon, King Zedekiah will die in captivity. Yet the evil which Zedekiah did in breaking his oath was not just against Nebuchadnezzar. The oath which Zedekiah swore he swore in the name of the Lord; therefore, he was also breaking his oath to God. Because of this, the judgment of God will come upon him, his army will be slain or scattered, and he will go to Babylon as a captive.

Yet the Lord ends this word with a note of hope. The Lord Himself will also take one of the highest branches and take a twig and plant it on a high mountain. And it will become the most majestic tree in the world and all the other

trees will know that the Lord is the God of the trees. The trees
in this final word represent all the nations. And the twig which
the Lord will plant is the Messiah, and He shall reign over all
the earth—for the Lord has spoken it.

Read Ezekiel chapter 15.

About what material does the Lord question Ezekiel?
(v. 2) What does it represent? (v. 6)

What is the point of God's questioning?

What is the wood of the vine good for? (v. 4)

What are the two fires in verse 7?

Why is God bringing this judgment on Jerusalem? (v. 8)

In this brief parable the Lord likens the inhabitants of
Jerusalem to the wood of the vine. And He is laborious in
pointing out that the wood of the vine is useless for anything
but fuel. He even goes on to say that if the wood of the vine
was not good for anything before it was burned, how much
less will it be useful after it is charred.

With these harsh words the Lord condemns the inhabitants of Jerusalem. He says they are good for nothing but the
fire; therefore, He is giving them up to judgment. The fire of
famine and pestilence will devour the people during the siege,
and those who escape with their lives will be pursued by the
judgments mentioned in Ezekiel's first acted prophecy.

A PROVERB REFUTED

Read Ezekiel 18.

Where else did we see this proverb refuted? What does this tell you?

With what general principle does the Lord begin the discussion of this proverb? (v. 4)

What is the relationship of the men discussed in verses 5–18?

What deeds does the first man do which show that he is righteous? (vv. 5–9)

What wicked deeds does the second man do? (vv. 10–13)

Restate verses 21 to 23 in your own words.

What will happen to the righteous man who falls into sin? (v. 24)

What is Israel's response to God's ways? (v. 25)

What is the great desire of God expressed in this chapter? What verses state this desire?

In this chapter we see the same proverb refuted which we saw in Jeremiah 31; this shows us that this saying was widespread among both the exiles and the people who had remained in the land. The proverb said, "The fathers have eaten sour grapes, and the children's teeth are set on edge" (v. 2); and Ezekiel spends much more time discussing this proverb than Jeremiah did.

The Lord begins by stating that every soul belongs to Him, and the soul that sins will die. He then proceeds to explain this by examining three generations of men. The first man is righteous. This man will live because he has been righteous before God.

However, the righteous man had a wicked son. The son practiced all of those sins which his father avoided. He also avoided the duties which his father practiced. This man will die because of his *own* sin; he cannot inherit the righteousness of his father. Yet that man also had a son. And his son saw the evil which his father did and turned away from it. Therefore he will live; he will not die for the sins of his father.

PROBING THE DEPTHS

This passage has great bearing on one of the biggest theological arguments in existence: the question of our sinning in Adam. The traditional Calvinist posture, which actually originated with St. Augustine, is that we each sinned in Adam, and we, therefore, bear the guilt of Adam's sin. The major text used in support of this position is Romans 5:12.

Against this position is the Arminian position which holds that the fall of man had a devastating effect on the image of God in man. Thus, in our fallen state we have an irreversible propensity to sin, and the image of God has been shattered, but we are guilty for our own sin—not for Adam's.

The message of this chapter gives strong support for the Arminian position. God clearly says that the soul that sins shall die, and one shall not die for the sin of his father.

The Lord explains that if the wicked turn away from their sin and repent, then they will live. God does not take pleasure in judging the wicked, but He desires that they repent and live. However, God's justice also demands that the righteous who turns to evil be judged, and he shall die because of his sins.

The Lord states and restates these principles, yet the people of Israel don't seem to get it. They say the Lord is not fair, yet the Lord will judge each person on the basis of his or her deeds. The message which repeatedly echoes though this chapter is "Turn and live!" (vv. 23, 30, 32).

 FAITH ALIVE

In this lesson we have seen that God repeatedly spoke to the Exiles about the necessity to turn away from sin. Their sin, and the continuing sin of the people remaining in Judah, was bringing the certainty of judgment to Jerusalem. Yet God again gives hope. "Turn and live!" is His cry to Israel, and to **all** people. He has promised that He will forgive and receive the penitent sinner.

Lesson 10/Trusting the Lord of Time
(Ezekiel 25—26; 28—29)

Pride is an endemic human characteristic. We can sermonize about it, we deplore it (particularly in other people), we even joke about it. But throughout the history of mankind we see the scars which have resulted from individual and corporate pride. In this lesson we are looking at prophecies of judgment against nations outside of Judah, but we will see that the pride of the rulers, or the pride of the nation, leads to judgment and destruction. And in studying these prophecies, we will not only see the problems brought about by pride, we will find that the Bible has the answer to pride as well.

THE PROPHECY AGAINST TYRE

Read Ezekiel 26.

Why is the Lord going to judge Tyre? (v. 2)

What three things does the Lord say He will do in verse 4?

Who will the Lord bring against Tyre? (v. 7)

What pronouns are used in verses 7–11?

What pronouns are used in verse 12?

What declaration is made in verse 14 which is similar to verses 4 and 5?

The prophecy against Tyre is one of the most dramatic examples of fulfilled prophecy in the Old Testament. The city was built in two parts: A portion of the city was on the mainland, and part of the city was on an island about one-half mile off-shore.

In 572 B.C. Nebuchadnezzar of Babylon conquered the city on the mainland (see Ezek. 29:18), but he was unable to take the island part of the city. Two hundred forty years later (332 B.C.) Alexander the Great set out to conquer the island city. His army built a causeway from the mainland to the island, using the debris from the site of the mainland city. This fulfilled Ezekiel's word (26:14).

The Lord declares judgment against Tyre because Tyre believes that she can capitalize on Jerusalem's fall and become richer and more powerful. The Lord declares that He will destroy the walls and towers of the city of Tyre. Furthermore, He will "scrape her dust from her, and make her like the top of a rock" (v. 4). This literally happened when Alexander the Great took the city.

THE FALL OF SATAN

In his word against the king of Tyre, Ezekiel, by the inspiration of the Holy Spirit, shifts from speaking about the literal king of Tyre to speaking about Satan and how he became proud and was cast down. This is one of two passages in the Old Testament which speak of the fall of Satan. The other, Isaiah 14, is also an oracle against a king—the king of Babylon.

Read Ezekiel 28 and Isaiah 14:12–15. What does the king of Tyre say he is? What does God say he is? (28:2)

What quality or characteristic of the king of Tyre is noted in verses 3–5?

How has the king of Tyre increased his wealth? (28:4, 5)

How will God judge the king of Tyre? (28:6–8)

Why will God judge the king of Tyre? (28:6)

In what verse does Ezekiel begin to speak of Satan rather than the king of Tyre? What indicates that Satan, rather than the king of Tyre, is being spoken of? (28:11–15)

What characteristics of Satan are spoken of before his fall? (28:12–15)

What things contributed to Satan's sin? (28:15–18)

How does God destroy Satan in Ezekiel 28:18?

What is Satan called in the Isaiah passage? (14:12)

What was the sin of Satan according to the Isaiah passage? (14:13, 14) How does this compare with the Ezekiel passage?

How does God destroy Satan in Isaiah? (14:15)

When did the fall of Satan occur?

What other city is prophesied about in this chapter of Ezekiel? (28:21)

Why is this city judged? (28:21–24)

What blessing is prophesied for Israel? (28:25, 26)

When will it come to pass? (28:25)

How does this blessing fit into this portion of Ezekiel?

The king of Tyre says, "I am a god," echoing Lucifer's words in Isaiah, "I will be like the Most High" (Is. 14:14). Yet God says to him, "You are a man, and not a god" (Ezek. 28:2). The king of Tyre was a smart businessman who had increased his wealth. Yet his glory was also his downfall, for the Bible tells us that his heart was lifted up because of his riches (28:5). Here we see another example of the foolishness of one "who lays up treasure for himself, and is not rich toward God" (Luke 12:21).

The pride which is spoken of here was also manifest in Satan; thus, this is a natural setup to speak of Satan and his pride. The transition comes in verse 11 with the break in the prophecy indicated by "moreover." Ezekiel is not talking about a mere human. Verse 13 says, "You were in Eden," and in verse 14 the subject of the prophecy is called "the anointed cherub who covers." Under the Holy Spirit's moving, Ezekiel is now speaking of a created spiritual being who worshiped before the throne of God at the earliest beginnings of creation.

The picture we see of the "anointed cherub" before his fall is one of wisdom and beauty. He was splendid, with a glittering covering of every precious stone, and perfection marked his ways. Yet he sinned when he rebelled against God and spread his rebellion among the heavenly hosts (Rev. 12:4).

The other thing which contributed to Satan's fall was his pride in his beauty: "You corrupted your wisdom for the sake of your splendor" (v. 17). This statement shows us the seduction of beauty. Satan allowed his wisdom to falter in lifting up his own beauty. We need both reason and beauty to live as God would have us to live, because we are to become like Him—and He created all that is good, and true, and beautiful.

The destruction of Satan comes from within. It is indeed God who destroys Satan, but He does it by bringing fire from within Satan himself. One might say that the violence with which Satan filled himself broke out into fire.

In Isaiah's account of the fall of Satan, we find some interesting contrasts, but no contradictions. Rather, Isaiah's perspective helps us to round out our picture of this cosmic event. Satan is called Lucifer in Isaiah, and indeed, that was his name before he fell. Lucifer means "Day Star"; this name refers to his high position in the heavenly host before his fall. Satan means "enemy," which is what he is now—an enemy to everything and everybody.

Satan's two chief sins were pride and rebellion, two sins which are frequently together. These two sins are the roots behind all sin. Pride causes us to put ourselves first, and rebellion causes us to think we can refuse God and disobey His commandments.

In the remainder of Ezekiel 28, the prophet speaks against Sidon, and he speaks a blessing upon Israel. Sidon was another seaport north of Tyre. With the fall of Tyre, Sidon became more important, but God also calls for judgment upon Sidon.

Israel's blessing is a promise to bring the people back to the land of Israel and establish them in safety. This promise may have related to the end of the captivity, and it may also be fulfilled in the future. God is assuring Israel that their promised land will be a secure possession as He judges their enemies and removes all cause for stumbling.

PROPHECIES AGAINST OTHER NATIONS

Read Ezekiel 25 and answer these questions.

Against what nations does Ezekiel prophesy? (vv. 2, 8, 12, 15)

What is the common element in the reason that God is judging these nations?

Against what nations will the Lord bring "the men of the East"? Where are these nations located? Who are the "men of the East"? (vv. 4, 10)

Against which nation does the Lord make two proclamations of judgment? (vv. 1–7)

Who is judged because of "old hatred"? (v. 15) Think about the term "old hatred." What does it mean? How can this apply to you and me? What can we learn from this passage regarding "old hatred"? What other Scriptures can you think of which may apply?

In this brief chapter Ezekiel gives words of judgment against four nations: Ammon, Moab, Edom, and Philistia. Interestingly enough, these nations were all among Judah's immediate neighbors, and the reason God was judging them centered on the way in which they each mistreated Judah and the people of Judah when Jerusalem was conquered. We all face the temptation to gloat over our enemies when defeat or some other misfortune befalls them. But Jesus taught us to "love your enemies, bless those who curse you, do good to those who hate you, and pray for those who spitefully use you and persecute you" (Matt. 5:44).

FAITH ALIVE

Look up the following references and tell how each applies to the present discussion.

Matthew 5:21–24

Matthew 6:9–15

Matthew 18:21–35

Ephesians 4:26, 27

PROPHECY AGAINST EGYPT

Read Ezekiel chapter 29.

What river is referred to in verse 3?

What declaration does Pharaoh make regarding the river? (v. 3)

What will happen to Pharaoh? (v. 5)

For what two reasons is Egypt going to be judged? (vv. 6, 9)

For how long will Egypt be judged? (v. 11) Is that figure literal or symbolic?

What will happen after forty years?

What political power or position will Egypt have after that time? (v. 15)

Why did Nebuchadnezzar not receive wages for his labor against Tyre? (See the second page of this lesson.)

What will Nebuchadnezzar now receive for wages? (v. 19) Why? (v. 20)

To what does verse 21 refer?

Ezekiel 29 through 32 contain several oracles against Egypt, with the common thread being the judgment of Egypt by the hand of Babylonia.

There are two reasons that the Lord is bringing this judgment. First, Egypt had been an unreliable ally to Judah (vv. 6, 7). Throughout the years that Judah was resisting Babylonian rule, the Judeans had put their trust in Egypt, and Egypt had failed them. Egypt failed, not because her army was not great enough, but because she did not trust in the Lord.

This point has important ramifications for us. When we are facing problems or trials—especially ones which look too big for us—we **must** turn to God. If we fail, it will be because of a lack of trust in God. If we trust the Lord, then even perceived failure will become a success.

The second and even more significant reason that Egypt was judged was because of the pride of Pharaoh in declaring that the river was his and he made it (v. 9). Here again, as with the king of Tyre, we see a man grasping for the place of God. But God will not give His glory to another (Is. 42:8), and pride will always bring destruction (Prov. 16:18).

With Egypt's fall, the Lord says He will cause "the horn of the house of Israel to spring forth" (v. 21).

WORD WEALTH

Horn, *qeren* (*keh*-ren); A horn of an animal; a flask or coronet; a symbol of strength, power, and victory. This noun occurs more than seventy-five times. Horned animals, such as oxen, goats, and rams, are symbols of strength. Thus Hebrew speakers refer to a person's horn's (sic) being exalted (Ps. 89:24; 112:9; 148:14), or contrarily, picture defeat as the breaking of the horn (Lam. 2:3). The "horns of the altar" (Lev. 4:7; 9:9; Ps. 118:27) are symbolic of the powerful presence of God. The root from which *qeren* comes is *qaran* "to have horns," "to shine." In Exodus 34:29, 30, 35, Moses' face shone, speaking of the projecting rays of glory that streamed from Moses' face.[1]

In the immediate historical context, the "horn of the house of Israel" was cut off when Jerusalem fell (see Lam. 2:3). Therefore, this reference is not necessarily messianic even though the term "horn" is sometimes used in messianic contexts (see Luke 1:69).

In Ezekiel 29:21 the "horn" spoken of springs forth with the fall of Egypt. Consequently, we can understand this term as messianic only in the broad context of referring to salvation. The Lord is saying that when Egypt falls His people will put their trust in Him rather than in man. This will become their source and symbol of power and strength, and then they shall know the Lord.

 FAITH ALIVE

This lesson has spoken much about God's judgment upon pride, yet it is fitting that we end by being called upon to trust the Lord. Trusting God is a means of turning from pride, for the essence of pride is believing that we don't need anyone other than ourselves. By putting our trust in the Lord, we are declaring our dependence on Him. We are saying that we *cannot* make it on our own; we *do* need God to help us.

Look up the following verses from Proverbs that deal with trust and pride. Comment on what these verses tell you, and focus, in particular, on personal application.

Proverbs 13:10

Proverbs 16:18

Proverbs 28:25

Proverbs 29:23

Proverbs 29:25

1. *Spirit-Filled Life® Bible* (Nashville: Thomas Nelson Publishers, 1991), 1198, "Word Wealth: Ezek. 29:21, horn."

Lesson 11/Patient Hope in God's Faithfulness
(Ezekiel 34—39)

One of the nice things about working a jigsaw puzzle is watching the picture take shape. As the various pieces come together you can see how different parts which you have worked on fit into the big picture. And it's nice to see your work begin to look like the picture on the box.

The study of these books is similar. Sometimes the pieces look chaotic, sometimes it's hard to see how different parts fit together, sometimes it seems like we're missing a piece. But as we begin to connect more of the pieces together, it begins to look like the "big picture" which is God's plan of redemption.

In this lesson from Ezekiel, we will put in some of those pieces which show God's love and mercy, for we will see God as the Shepherd, and as the Restorer and Defender of His people.

THE TRUE SHEPHERD

Read Ezekiel 34.

Who are the shepherds of Israel? (vv. 2–10)

What six things are the shepherds accused of in verse 4?

What were the results of the shepherds' negligence? (vv. 5, 6)

What is the word of the Lord to the shepherds? What will be their penalty? (vv. 7–10)

Who will be the new shepherd? (vv. 11–16)

What does the "cloudy and dark day" of verse 12 refer to?

How will God provide for His sheep? (vv. 13–15)

Who else does God judge in this chapter? (v. 20)

What have the "fat sheep" done? (v. 18)

Who will God assign as shepherd? Who does this represent? (vv. 23, 24)

What blessings will the Lord bring to His flock? (vv. 25–29)

This passage is a gracious expression of God's care for His people, yet "judgment must begin at the house of God" (1 Pet. 4:17, KJV), so God begins by speaking against the "shepherds of Israel." God uses a shepherd/sheep metaphor throughout this prophecy, and the shepherds who are spoken against are the leaders of Israel.

The shepherds of Israel did not strengthen the weak or care for the sick and injured. They failed to seek the lost or bring back that which was driven off. Rather, they used the flock only for their own enrichment.

But the Lord is always watching over His flock, and He has serious words for the shepherds. He will require the flock at their hand—they will have to answer for the damage which was done and the sheep which were lost through their negligence or irresponsibility. Furthermore, God will remove them from their positions as shepherds.

Then God Himself will be the Shepherd, and He will seek for His sheep and save them and care for them. He provides everything for His sheep which the bad shepherds were not providing: He *will* strengthen the weak and care for the sick and injured. We need to hear the heart of God in this passage. He cares for us, and wishes to bind up what is broken in our lives and make our weakness into strength.

In addition to the inadequate shepherds, the Lord also speaks against the "fat sheep"—the well off and healthy ones who showed no consideration for the small and weak. In the pastoral imagery of this word, the fat sheep have overgrazed the good pastures and then trampled what little grass remained. They drank of the clear, clean water and then they carelessly muddied the waters with their feet. Therefore, the Lord will also judge between the sheep, and He will ensure that none of His flock become prey—either to the beasts or to the stronger sheep who would use their size and strength to defraud the weak.

The Lord will accomplish these things by appointing David to be the shepherd. This is a clear reference to the Lord Jesus. How does Jesus prevent the fat sheep from abusing the lean sheep? As shepherd and Lord, He is in control of the flock and He will do what He needs to do in order to prevent abuse. The Shepherd Himself has also become our example.

By coming to earth and showing us how to live, He set a standard for the sheep to follow.

THE RESTORATION OF ISRAEL

Read Ezekiel 35 and 36.

What country is indicated when Ezekiel speaks of Mount Seir? (35:2)

Why is the Lord judging Mount Seir? (35:5) (See Lam. 4:21; Obad. 10–14.)

What will be the judgment upon Mount Seir? (35:6–9)

What phrases in 36:1–8 connect chapters 35 and 36? (36:1, 4, 5)

The Lord says, " Because you have borne the _____ ____ nations . . . the nations that are around you shall _____ _____ _____ _____." (36:6, 7)

How did the nations taunt Israel? (36:13, 14)

Why did God pour out His fury upon Israel? (36:18)

How is the statement of verse 20 negative?

Why is God going to bring back Israel to its land? (36:22–24)

What will God do for the people after bringing them back to the land? (36:24–30)

What will be the response of the people when they remember their sins? (36:31) Comment.

The Lord says that He will increase Israel "like a flock offered as holy sacrifices." What does this mean? (36:38)

Chapters 35 and 36 form a single oracle which concerns the restoration of Israel. Yet the prophecy begins with a word of judgment against Mount Seir, the capital city of Edom. When Jerusalem fell, the Edomites assisted the Babylonians in hunting down fugitives and plundering the city (see Obad. 12–14). Because of this, the Lord will judge Edom and make Mount Seir a desolation.

God had poured out His fury upon Israel because of their sin, and because of their disobedience He had judged them and scattered them. However, the nations to which they traveled thought the Lord was powerless to protect them. So the nations were mocking God when they said, "These are Yahweh's people, and they have gone out of the land."

Therefore, God will bring back Israel in order to sanctify His name. It is not because the children of Israel are good, nor because they deserve blessing because they paid for their sin, but because the Lord will be hallowed when the nations see the blessing He brings to Israel in bringing them back to their land.

Then, when they have returned, the Lord will cleanse them and put a new spirit within them. He will cause them to walk in His ways and keep His statutes. This is the greatest blessing we can receive: to be transformed within and to be made able to follow God.

The Lord says He will increase Israel "like a flock offered as a holy sacrifice." Now this could be misconstrued as a way of saying that God is going to fatten us up for the kill. But what God is actually saying is that the people will be multiplied to be as numerous as the flocks which were brought to Jerusalem when there was a great feast day. On those feasts, when people came from all over the country to offer sacrifices, the flocks which were brought to Jerusalem were huge! And God is saying that the multiplication of the people will also be huge. His blessings will bring abundance to all areas of life, and the people will know that He is the Lord.

THE VALLEY OF DRY BONES

Read Ezekiel 37.

Where does God take Ezekiel? (v. 1)

In light of the interpretation of this vision, what is the meaning of the dryness of the bones? (v. 2)

WORD WEALTH

Spirit, *ruach* (*roo*-ach); Spirit, wind, breath. This word occurs nearly 400 times. Job 37:21 and Ps. 148:8 speak about "winds" related to storms. In Genesis 6:17, "the *ruach* of life" is translated "the breath of life." Generally *ruach* is translated "spirit," whether concerning the human spirit, a distressing spirit (1 Sam. 16:23), or the Spirit of God. The Holy Spirit is especially presented in Isaiah: God puts His Spirit upon the Messiah (42:1); He will pour out His Spirit upon Israel's descendants (44:3); Yahweh and His Spirit both send the Anointed One (48:16, a reference to the triune God); the Spirit of God commissions and empowers the Messiah (61:1–3); see also 59:19, 21.[1]

Now comment on the use of the terms breath, wind, and spirit in this prophecy (vv. 8–10, 14).

What would have been the primary meaning of this prophecy to Ezekiel's audience?

In the second oracle in this chapter, what does the Lord tell Ezekiel to do?

What is the meaning of the second prophecy?

How do these two prophecies connect with each other?

The vision of the valley of dry bones is one of the most famous in the Book of Ezekiel. God takes Ezekiel into a valley full of bones, and the bones are very dry. The dryness of these bones show that they have been dead a long, long time. And God asks Ezekiel, "Can these bones live?" (v. 3).

The dryness of the bones is an indication of Israel's hope (see v. 11). Israel's hope was not just dead, it had been dead for a while—long enough for any chance of revival of hope to have been extinguished. So Israel faced what you and I face— dead hope. We each have hopes which have been given up so long ago that we see no chance of the hope's fulfillment. But notice Ezekiel's response. Recognizing that almighty God is asking the question, he answers, "O Lord GOD, You know." When we are dealing with dead hopes, the best thing we can do is leave them in the Lord's hands.

Ezekiel is then commanded to prophesy to the bones, and the bones come together and are covered with muscle and flesh, yet there was no spirit in them. The Lord tells Ezekiel to prophesy to the *ruach* and say come from the four *ruachs*. And in verse 14 God says He will put His *ruach* or Spirit in Israel.

So ultimately, this prophecy was a message of hope to a hopeless group of exiles. It is also a message of hope to us. And the source of the hope in both cases is the Spirit of God. We may be dead, and our hopes may have withered, but the Holy Spirit—who can breathe life into the dead, and who is the giver of life—He can revive hope as well.

The Lord also tells Ezekiel to take two sticks, write "Judah" on one, and "Israel" on the other and join them together. This may communicate an obvious message to us, but the children of Israel needed an interpretation. So the Lord says through Ezekiel that the two sundered nations, which had been split for about four hundred years, would again be united and would never be separated again. And this promise is confirmed with the promises that the Messiah would rule, the tabernacle would be among them (indicating restored worship), and God Himself would be their God. God's plan is to bring perfect restoration to every element which has fallen.

THE PROPHECY CONCERNING GOG

Read Ezekiel 38 and 39.

In 38:1–10 what is the main activity taking place? How does God indicate that He is in control?

What is the condition of Israel at the time the prophecy takes place? (38:11)

What do Gog and his allies plan to do? (38:12, 13)

What will God do in judging Gog? What will be the result of Gog's defeat? (38:18–23)

In 39:1–8 what is being emphasized about God's judgment on Gog? Why is this emphasized?

How long will the people be burning Gog's weapons? (39:9) How long will they be burying the dead? (39:12)

Why will there be a thorough search for bones? (39:14, 15)

Compare 39:17–20 with Revelation 19:17–21. Comment.

When the Lord sets His glory among the nations, what will Israel then know? What will the Gentiles know? (39:21–24)

This prophecy shows how God is in control of the nations, how He will protect His people, and how He will bring the final victory of righteousness.

In this prophecy against Gog, we see that Gog will prepare a great army. He and his allies, with all of their troops, will come into the land of Israel like a storm cloud. But the Lord is orchestrating these events. He has put hooks into the jaws of Gog (v. 4), and He is leading him where He wants him to go.

When judgment falls on Gog there will be a great earthquake, and pestilence, and bloodshed. The Lord also will rain down fire, and brimstone, and great hailstones. These are all figures which are also seen by John in his apocalyptic visions, and they are signs that the day of the lord—that final day of judgment—is coming upon the earth. Thus, this prophecy speaks not only of the end of some distant enemy of national Israel, but of the end of all of God's enemies, and of His overthrow of the present evil age.

The Lord will set His glory among the nations, and Israel will know that He is their God, and that He was in control of their destiny all along. The nations will also know that He is God, and they will understand something of the righteousness and justice of God, for they will see that Israel went into captivity and was scattered because of their sin.

 FAITH ALIVE

God is faithful to protect and bless His people now, and in their immediate future, and to the end of the age. Ezekiel was prophesying to exiles who had been taken captive to a distant land. It probably didn't seem like they were receiving a blessing at the time. But in the midst of the exile, the Lord was still speaking to these people and protecting them. God's faithfulness in protecting and blessing us sometimes appears to take strange forms. Joseph's experience as a slave in Egypt (Gen. 39—47) did not seem like a blessing at the time, but later he told his brothers, "God sent me before you . . . to save your lives" (Gen. 45:7).God uses all things in our lives to bless us and conform us into His image.

1. *Spirit-Filled Life® Bible* (Nashville: Thomas Nelson Publishers, 1991), 474, "Word Wealth: 2 Sam. 23:2, Spirit."

Lesson 12/Trusting in the Ultimate Hope
(Ezekiel 40—48)

Throughout these lessons the temple of the Lord has figured prominently in many ways. The people of Jerusalem said, "The temple of the Lord, the temple of the Lord, the temple of the Lord" (Jer. 7:4), yet Jeremiah said they were trusting in lying words. The temple was not a good luck charm which could keep away evil by its mere presence. Yet it was the Lord's desire to purify the people and restore pure worship. So it is fitting that in this last lesson we study Ezekiel's vision of the new temple which symbolizes perfected and purified worship.

THE VISION OF THE TEMPLE

Read Ezekiel 40—44. Pay particular attention to chapters 43 and 44.

When did Ezekiel have this vision? What is significant about that time?

How long was the rod that man used to measure with?

Where does the angel start his measuring of the temple? Is there any significance to this?

In Ezekiel 40:20–37 what is being measured? What message is being communicated by the amount of time given to these? What is important about them being identical?

What geometric shape is prominent in these descriptions? What is being said in this?

Compare 43:1–5 with 10:18, 19. Comment.

What promise does God make in 43:7–9? What is the condition of the promise?

Why did God tell Ezekiel to describe the temple? Why would this description have the effect God is looking for?

In Ezekiel 43:27, what happens on the eighth day? What is a New Testament parallel to the eighth day?

Many people speak of Ezekiel 44:1, 2 as being a fulfilled prophecy. How has it supposedly been fulfilled? Do you agree with this interpretation? Why?

In Ezekiel 44:6–9, what does the Lord upbraid the children of Israel for?

What is the significance of not allowing the "uncircumcised in heart and uncircumcised in flesh" to come into the temple?

What does verse 8 say to you?

What promise is given to the Levites who strayed from the Lord? What is forbidden to them?

What will be the duties of the priests and Levites who did not stray from the Lord?

Why do the priests wear linen? What is the point behind that reason?

Ezekiel's vision begins by being transported to a "very high mountain" and seeing something like a city. The Lord then takes him to the gateway of this structure, which is the new temple, and hands him over to an angel who will be his guide through this temple. The angel has a rod which is six cubits long, but these cubits are larger than the "normal" cubit. Each of these "long" cubits (sometimes called the "royal" cubit) is about twenty and one-half inches long, making the rod about ten feet three inches long (3.1 meters).

The guide takes Ezekiel and begins measuring the eastern gate of the temple area. This gate has particular significance for two reasons: first, as we will see, the glory of the Lord returns through the eastern gate, second, the eastern gate will be shut (sealed up) as it is today—a fact with prophetic significance.

After measuring the eastern gate, the guide takes Ezekiel into the temple's outer court and they measure the court and the other gateways. They also measure the gateways into the inner court, and they find that all the gates are identical. The point is that the way to God is controlled and guarded. Those who come into this new temple must be true worshipers. The indistinguishable nature of the gates show us that we must come to God His way. Also, the identical gates point out the perfection of the new temple. In the same way, the recurrence of the square shape in the temple (the gate chambers, the inner court, and the entire temple complex) indicates the perfection of this temple. The following diagram will help you visualize it.

 ## AT A GLANCE

EZEKIEL'S TEMPLE[1]

Ezekiel's restored temple is not a blueprint, but a vision that stresses the purity and spiritual vitality of the ideal place of worship and those who will worship there. It is not intended for an earthly, physical fulfillment, but expresses the truth found in the name of the new city: "THE LORD *IS* THERE" (Ezek. 48:35). God will dwell in the new temple and among His people.

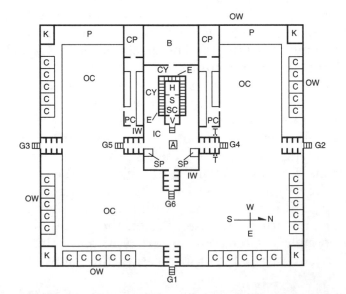

The Temple Complex

OW	Wall of outer court (40:5)		SP	Chambers for singers and priests (40:44–46)
G1	Eastern outer gateway (40:6–16)		A	Altar (40:47; 43:13–27)
OC	Outer court (40:17)		V	Vestibule of temple (40:48, 49)
C	Chambers in outer court (40:17)		S	Sanctuary or holy place (41:1, 2)
P	Pavement (40:17, 18)		H	Most Holy Place (41:3, 4)
G2	Northern outer gateway (40:20–22)		SC	Side chambers (41:5–7)
G4	Northern inner gateway (40:23, 35–37)		E	Elevation around temple (41:8)
			CY	Separating courtyard (41:20)
G3	Southern outer gateway (40:24–26)		B	Building at west end (41:12)
G5	Southern inner gateway (40:27–31)		PC	Priest's chambers (42:1–14)
IC	Inner court (40:32)		IW	Wall of inner court (42:10)
G6	Eastern inner gateway (40:32–34)		CP	Priest's cooking places (46:19, 20)
T	Tables for killing sacrifices (40:38–43)		K	Kitchens (46:21–24)

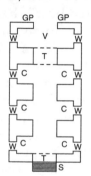

The Gateway

S	Steps (40:6)
T	Thresholds (40:6, 7)
C	Gate chambers (40:7, 10, 12)
W	Windows (40:16)
V	Vestibule (40:8, 9)
GP	Gateposts (40:10, 14)

Having accepted the people back into fellowship with Him, God now commands that only those in covenant relationship with Him be admitted to the temple. He rebukes the children of Israel for allowing foreigners into the temple (44:6, 7). But does not the Lord wish for His house to be "a house of prayer for all people"? (Isa. 56:7; Mark 11:17). Yes, of course He does. But His rebuke here in Ezekiel is further qualified by the phrase "uncircumcised in heart and uncircumcised in flesh." The people whom the Lord does not want in His temple are those who are not truly repentant and those who are not ready to commit totally to Him.

This is also a change from the attitudes of the people which are condemned in verse 8. God says that they did not keep the temple but allowed others to do the job for them. This verse again speaks of the individual responsibility which is taught prominently throughout Ezekiel. We cannot allow others to do the work of God for us.

After speaking of the worshipers, we turn to consider the ministers in the temple. The Levites who strayed from the Lord will be restored and will have a place of ministry in the new temple; this shows us the willingness of God to forgive and accept the sinful ones.

The message about the eastern gate being closed is considered to be messianic by many people. The interpretation is that the glory of the Lord entered Jerusalem via the eastern gate when the Lord Jesus went into Jerusalem on Palm Sunday. It was hundreds of years later that a Turkish ruler heard that the Messiah would enter the city through that gate, so he ordered the gate to be sealed up. And so it is that, to this day, the eastern gate remains walled up "because the Lord God has entered by it" (Ezek. 44:2).

However, it must also be noted that, in the immediate context of this passage, the glory of the Lord *did* enter the temple by the eastern gate, and that is to what this reference directly alludes. But we must keep in mind the nature of this vision and the nature of prophecy. This vision is a symbolic representation of God's plan to restore pure worship. Therefore, for the vision to include a reference to a historic event within the story of redemption is consistent with the purpose of the message as a whole. In addition, the nature of prophecy allows for there to be multiple fulfillments of a single prophecy. So both the character of this message and the nature of prophecy allow for this verse to be understood as the direct result of the entrance of the glory of God in chapter 43, and as the result of the Lord's entrance into Jerusalem 600 years later.

THE VISION OF THE LAND

Read Ezekiel 45, 46, and 47:13—48:35.

What is the first district in the land to be apportioned? What message can we derive from this fact? (45:1–5)

How long is the holy district? What is the measurement in miles?

Is the allotment of land to the prince larger or smaller than the holy district? (45:6)

What three commands does the Lord give to the princes? (45:9–17)

In what ways does the Lord provide for the prince? What are the religious duties of the prince?

When would the eastern gate of the inner court be opened? Why? (46:1–3)

How shall the prince provide for his sons' inheritance? What is explicitly forbidden? (46:16–18)

What inheritance is provided for the strangers which dwell with the Israelites? How does this apply to us? (47:22–23)

Where is the holy district in relationship to the land as a whole? Where is the sanctuary in relationship to the holy district? What is God trying to tell us by this arrangement? (48:8)

How many gates does the city have? (48:30–34) What are their names? What does John add in his description of the city in Revelation 21:10–21?

Which city is larger, John's or Ezekiel's? What does this tell you about interpreting these passages? What is the name of Ezekiel's city? (48:35)

Ezekiel's vision of the land is actually a set of instructions to apportion the land. The twelve tribes were to divide the land, with each tribe getting an equal portion. However, before any of the tribes were considered, the portion of the land set apart for God and the temple was dealt with. In this order we are reminded of the presenting of firstfruits and tithes—the Lord receives His portion first. By asking us to acknowledge Him first, God is insuring that we will remain open to the flow of life which He provides.

Notice that the prince is given a section of land which is much larger than the holy district, and with that land comes the instruction that the prince must not oppress the people (45:8).

Another group mentioned in these chapter is the foreigners. These foreigners were people who had settled and begun a new life in the midst of the people of God. They had left their own lands and families to be part of God's people; consequently, they were given an inheritance by God.

This is a great promise to us who have come to the Lord. We were foreigners, "aliens from the commonwealth of Israel and strangers from the covenants of promise, having no hope and without God in the world" (Eph. 2:12). But God has promised to accept us and to provide us with an inheritance with His people. This is a beautiful Old Testament example of the universality of the plan of God.

When Ezekiel describes the actual allotment of the land, we find that the holy district is in the center of the land, and the sanctuary is in the center of the holy district. Just as God wants us to put Him first, likewise, He should be central in our lives.

Finally, Ezekiel gives us a few details about the city itself. Like the city which John sees in the Book of Revelation, Ezekiel's city has twelve gates named after the twelve tribes of Israel. However, John also sees that there are twelve foundations with the names of the twelve apostles. In addition, the city which John sees is much larger than the city which Ezekiel saw. The fact that there are important similarities, and yet some significant differences, should tell us that in both cases we are seeing symbolic representations of truth.

THE RIVER OF GOD

These books we have studied have told the sad story of rebellious people who will not turn to God. They have set themselves against God; therefore, God must set Himself against them in judgment. Accordingly, most of the study has not been joyful and uplifting. Yet, in spite of the heavy message, there is hope within these prophecies. In fact, both Jeremiah and Ezekiel contain lengthy sections which are messages of hope, and it is with one of these prophecies that this study ends.

Ezekiel's vision of the river of God is a brief prophecy, yet it contains an important message for us.

Read Ezekiel 47:1–12.

Where did the river start? (v. 1)

What happens as Ezekiel goes further down the river? (vv. 3–6)

In total, how far does the angel lead Ezekiel down the river? (vv. 3–6)

To what sea does the river flow?

What happens when the river reaches the sea? (v. 8)

Why are the marshes and swamps left salty? (v. 11)

What is the significance of the trees? (v. 12)

In this part of the vision Ezekiel is taken back to the temple, and he sees a river coming out from under the threshold of the temple. This figure is obviously stating that the origin of the river is God Himself. The river flows from the temple, out of the city and continues on to the east. Ezekiel follows the angel and the river gets deeper and deeper until it is finally deep enough to swim in.

This vision calls each of us to pursue what God has for us and to continue to follow His leading into deeper and deeper things. As we follow God we find that His truth that He leads us in, and His purpose for us both deepen. Yet as He leads us, He also gives us the ability to swim and to follow His leading as far as He wishes to take us.

This river flowed into the Dead Sea, and then the waters of the Dead Sea were healed and the sea could support life. The angel tells Ezekiel, "Everything will live wherever the river goes" (v. 9). This is a second reason to stay with the river: wherever the river of God goes, there is life!

Some have suggested that the swamps were left salty as a source of salt for human needs and for use in sacrifices. Yet they may stand in stagnant contrast to God's healing, flowing river.

Finally, the trees which Ezekiel sees are abundant in fruit and do not wither. John, in Revelation, identifies these trees as the tree of life. And they are indeed full of life! The thrust of this whole vision is life. Wherever God's river flows, He brings life, and the life He supplies is abundant. This vision of Ezekiel's is an invitation—an invitation to come and live in the river of God and partake of, and participate in, His life.

FAITH ALIVE

We have seen in this lesson that God desires restored worship. Indeed, all of God's plan is directed toward the restoration of relationship between God and man, and proper relationship between God and man entails worship.

Along with this restoration of worship is the restoration of proper relationship *between* people. The message of the division of the land is that all are equal, and those in positions of prominence or power are to carry out their responsibilities without taking advantage of others. It all comes down to *your* relationship with God. God wants to lead you deeper, and you will never drown in His river, for His river brings life.

What portion of this vision spoke most directly to you? Why?

In what area of your life is God taking you deeper currently?

1. *Spirit-Filled Life® Bible* (Nashville: Thomas Nelson Publishers, 1991), 1214, "Ezekiel's Temple: Ezek. 40:5."

SPIRIT-FILLED LIFE® BIBLE DISCOVERY GUIDE SERIES

B 1   Genesis 0-8407-8515-1
B 2   Exodus, Leviticus, Numbers, Deuteronomy
0-8407-8513-5
B 3   Joshua & Judges 0-7852-1242-6
B 4   Ruth & Esther 0-7852-1133-0
B 5   1 & 2 Samuel, 1 Chronicles 0-7852-1243-4
B 6   1 & 2 Kings, 2 Chronicles 0-7852-1257-4
B 7   Ezra & Nehemiah 0-7852-1258-2
B 8   Job, Ecclesiastes, Song of Songs 0-7852-1376-7
B 9   Psalms 0-8407-8347-7
B 10   Proverbs 0-7852-1167-5
B 11   Isaiah 0-7852-1168-3
B 12   Jeremiah, Lamentations, Ezekiel 0-7852-1377-5
B 13   Daniel & Revelation 0-8407-2081-5
B 14   Hosea, Joel, Amos, Obadiah, Jonah, Micah, Nahum,
Habakkuk, Zephaniah, Haggai, Zechariah, Malachi
0-8407-2093-9
B 15   Matthew, Mark, Luke 0-8407-2090-4
B 16   John 0-8407-8349-3
B 17   Acts 0-8407-8345-0
B 18   Romans 0-8407-8350-7
B 19   1 Corinthians 0-8407-8514-3
B 20   2 Corinthians, 1 & 2 Timothy, Titus 0-7852-1204-3
B 21   Galatians, 1 & 2 Thessalonians 0-7852-1134-9
B 22   Ephesians, Philippians, Colossians, Philemon
0-8407-8512-7
B 23   Hebrews 0-8407-2082-3
B 24   James, 1 & 2 Peter, 1–3 John, Jude 0-7852-1205-1
B 25   *Getting to the Heart of the Bible (Key Themes: Basics
of Bible Study)

*Coming Soon

SPIRIT-FILLED LIFE® KINGDOM DYNAMICS STUDY GUIDES

K 1 People of the Spirit: Gifts, Fruit, and Fullness of the Holy Spirit 0-8407-8431-7

K 2 Kingdom Warfare: Prayer, Spiritual Warfare, and the Ministry of Angels 0-8407-8433-3

K 3 God's Way to Wholeness: Divine Healing by the Power of the Holy Spirit 0-8407-8430-9

K 4 Life in the Kingdom: Foundations of the Faith 0-8407-8432-5

K 5 Focusing on the Future: Key Prophecies and Practical Living 0-8407-8517-8

K 6 Toward More Glorious Praise: Power Principles for Faith-Filled People 0-8407-8518-6

K 7 Bible Ministries for Women: God's Daughters and God's Work 0-8407-8519-4

K 8 People of the Covenant: God's New Covenant for Today 0-8407-8520-8

K 9 Answering the Call to Evangelism: Spreading the Good News to Everyone 0-8407-2096-3

K 10 Spirit-Filled Family: Holy Wisdom to Build Happy Homes 0-8407-2085-8

K 11 Appointed to Leadership: God's Principles for Spiritual Leaders 0-8407-2083-1

K 12 Power Faith: Balancing Faith in Words and Work 0-8407-2094-7

K 13 Race & Reconciliation: Healing the Wounds, Winning the Harvest 0-7852-1131-4

K 14 Praying in the Spirit: Heavenly Resources for Praise and Intercession 0-7852-1141-1

OTHER SPIRIT-FILLED LIFE® STUDY RESOURCES

Spirit-Filled Life® Bible, available in several bindings and in NKJV and KJV.
Spirit-Filled Life® Bible for Students
Hayford's Bible Handbook 0-8407-8359-0